the Spirit —
God in action

ANTHONY D. PALMA

GOSPEL PUBLISHING HOUSE
Springfield, Missouri
02-0602

contents

Contents

1

the Spirit and the Godhead

Who, or what, is the Holy Spirit? This question was not raised in the Apostolic Church. But within a few centuries it became necessary for the Christian Church to give attention to this matter. Some leaders in the Church were teaching that the Holy Spirit was created by the eternal Son of God and therefore could not be considered a member of the Godhead. This was actually a denial of the doctrine of the Trinity—that God exists eternally in three Persons whom we commonly designate as Father, Son, and Holy Spirit.

In this chapter we shall deal with two main topics—the personality of the Holy Spirit and the deity of the Holy Spirit. This will be followed by a brief survey of Early Church history as it relates to these matters.

THE PERSONALITY OF THE HOLY SPIRIT

The Scriptures clearly teach that the Holy Spirit is a personal being. Yet there is still some misunderstanding among Christians on this matter, so that they refer to the Spirit as *It* rather than *He*.

Reasons for This Confusion. Here are some of the main reasons for this misunderstanding:

1. He is the least mentioned of the three members of the Trinity. There are considerably more references in Scripture to the Father and the Son than there are to the Holy Spirit. Consequently, less is known about Him than about others.

2. The word *Spirit* suggests absence of personality. We have no difficulty in attaching the idea of personality to the words *Father* and *Son*; but in our language the word *Spirit* is neuter in gender, which means that the appropriate pronoun to be used is *It*. However, we shall see later that in spite of this accident of language there is abundant evidence in Scripture to prove that the Holy Spirit is a Person.

3. The Biblical languages are also partly responsible for this problem. Our word *Spirit* is a simple and valid translation of the Hebrew word *ruach* and the Greek word *pneuma*. These are common words in those languages. Their basic meaning is that of wind, breath, or air. In the English language, we have separate words for each of them. The Hebrew and Greek languages can use one word which has all of those meanings. Originally, the words *ruach* and *pneuma* were used for inanimate and impersonal forces like wind and breath. Later, the words were applied to what we understand by the word *spirit*. An interesting fact is that Hebrew has no neuter gender, and that the word for *spirit* is feminine in gender. Greek, on the other hand, uses the neuter gender in its word for *spirit*. The point of all this is to show that both in the Biblical languages and in English the doctrine of the Holy Spirit is sometimes misunderstood because of linguistic limitations.

4. Translations of the Bible are sometimes inadequate. This may be due to the translators' desire to give a "strict" translation, or to an unawareness of the overall

Biblical teaching about the Holy Spirit. For instance, Romans 8:26 in the King James Verson reads, "Likewise the Spirit also helpeth our infirmities, for we know not what we should pray for as we ought; but the Spirit *itself* maketh intercession for us with groanings which cannot be uttered." It is much better to follow the reading of the New American Standard Bible, for instance, which says " . . . the Spirit *Himself* . . . "

5. He is often associated in Scripture with the idea of power. Consequently there are some who think of the Holy Spirit in terms of an impersonal force. But when Jesus promised the disciples that they would receive power when the Holy Spirit came upon them (Acts 1:8; Luke 24:49), He meant that the Spirit himself would come in fullness and that the Spirit, who is all-powerful, would provide them with the necessary means for effective witnessing.

6. The figures of speech that are often used in Scripture for the Holy Spirit suggest the ideas of inanimate or impersonal objects. Only a few suggestions are necessary to illustrate this point. He is likened to:

Water—John 7:38, 39.

Oil—Acts 10:38. Throughout the Bible anointing is mentioned as being done with oil.

Wind—John 3:8; Acts 2:2.

Fire—Acts 2:3.

A dove—Luke 3:22.

These symbols of the Holy Spirit will receive further attention at appropriate points in the following chapters. Here it is simply necessary to state that a figure of speech is used to help us understand something about a person. If we say, "Pastor Jones is a real powerhouse for God," we do not mean that he is not a person. We are simply using an object from everyday life to express some characteristic or attribute of this person.

Proof of the Spirit's Personality. There are many lines of evidence in the Scriptures that point to the fact that the Holy Spirit is a Person and not an inanimate object or impersonal force. At this stage in our study, we are concerned primarily with establishing this fact by a survey of the material. We will give further treatment to many of these matters in subsequent chapters.

1. He possesses personal attributes. These are qualities that are associated with the mind, the will, and the emotions.

Paul speaks of "the mind of the Spirit" (Romans 8:27), and says further that only the Spirit of God knows the deep things of God (1 Corinthians 2:10, 11). The intellectual activity of the Holy Spirit is further seen in gifts of the Spirit such as a word of knowledge, a word of wisdom, discerning of spirits, and prophecy (1 Corinthians 12:8-10). Secondly, there is the matter of the will, or volition. One aspect of this is the sovereignty of the Holy Spirit. He distributes the gifts of the Spirit "to each one individually just as He wills" (1 Corinthians 12:11, NASB). He directs God's people in setting some apart for special ministry (Acts 13:2) and in the choice of fields of labor (Acts 16:6, 7). Finally, the Holy Spirit has emotions. The Spirit may be grieved or vexed (Ephesians 4:30; Isaiah 63:10). He manifests love (Romans 15:30).

2. He performs personal acts. It will be sufficient for us simply to list some of these, with a few appropriate Scripture references:

He creates—Genesis 1:2; Proverbs 33:6; Job 33:4.
He recreates, or regenerates—John 3:5; Titus 3:5.
He strives with men—Genesis 6:3; Isaish 63:10.

He convicts, or convinces, unregenerate men—John 16:8.

He intercedes—Romans 8:26.

He performs miracles—Hebrews 2:4; Acts 8:39.

He raises the dead—Romans 1:3, 4; 8:11.

He speaks—John 16:13; Acts 8:29; 10:19; Revelation 2:7.

He teaches—John 14:26; 1 John 2:27; Luke 12:12.

He testifies—John 15:26; 1 Peter 1:11.

3. He may be personally offended. Stephen charged his persecutors with always resisting the Holy Spirit (Acts 7:51). Peter accused Ananias of lying to the Holy Spirit (Acts 5:3) and further stated that both Ananias and Sapphira had put the Spirit of the Lord to the test (v. 9). Paul admonishes Christians not to grieve the Holy Spirit (Ephesians 4:30), probably recalling how Israel had so offended Him in the wilderness (Isaiah 63:10). Furthermore, believers are warned of the possibility of insulting or outraging "the Spirit of grace" by denying their blood-bought salvation (Hebrews 10:29). Then in one of the most solemn passages in all of Scripture, Jesus warns against blaspheming, or sinning against, the Holy Spirit (Matthew 12:22-32; Mark 3:22-30; Luke 12:10).

The precise nature of this sin is a subject of dispute among Biblical scholars, but at least two points are quite clear when we examine the entire context: (1) It consists of *knowingly* and *persistently* attributing to Satan what is obviously the work of the Holy Spirit; and (2) it is a rejection of Jesus Christ as God's chosen and anointed One for the deliverance of mankind. No Christian need be preoccupied or distressed with the thought that he has committed this sin. The very fact that he is concerned about it is clear indication that the Holy Spirit has not forsaken him!

4. Jesus called Him the Paraclete. This term is a transliteration of the Greek *Parakletos* and is translated variously as Comforter, Helper, Counselor, Advocate. Its root meaning is "one called to the side of." The passages where this title is found (John 14:16, 26; 15:26; 16:7) clearly indicate that Jesus is talking about the Holy Spirit as a Person. As we noticed earlier, the New Testament writers were forced to use a neuter noun when they spoke of the Spirit of God because there was no other choice. But when a choice was available, as between a neuter and a masculine form for Paraclete, they selected the masculine.

A further indication of the Spirit's personality is found in Jesus' words "another Paraclete" (John 14:16). Jesus himself was the first Paraclete. We are told by the apostle John that "we have an advocate [Paraclete] with the Father, Jesus Christ the righteous" (1 John 2:1). The clue is in the word *another*, which in the Greek normally means "another of the same kind." Just as the Lord Jesus Christ comes to the aid of His people and encourages them, so the Holy Spirit likewise helps, encourages, and intercedes for those who belong to Him. Jesus promised He would not leave His disciples as orphans—helpless, defenseless, comfortless (John 14:18)!

5. Masculine pronouns are used for the Holy Spirit. It seems that in a few passages Jesus deliberately emphasized the personality of the Spirit by using masculine forms of pronouns when He could either have omitted the pronoun as in John 14:26, where the word *He* could have been omitted without injury to the grammar) or where He could have used a neuter form (as in John 16:13, 14, where the neuter word *Spirit* is found).

THE DEITY OF THE HOLY SPIRIT

The Holy Spirit is a member of the Trinity, which

means that He is fully divine, like the Father and the Son. Following our discussion in the preceding section of this chapter, we may now confidently call Him the Third Person of the Godhead.

Scriptural Evidence for His Deity. There are many lines of evidence proving the absolute deity of the Holy Spirit. Here are the most important ones:

1. He is mentioned coordinately with the Father and the Son. The following examples demonstrate that all three are equal. Otherwise it would be a case of mixing the proverbial apples and oranges!

Jesus commanded the disciples to baptize believers "in the name of the Father and the Son and the Holy Spirit" (Matthew 28:19, NASB).

Paul, in three parallel phrases, speaks of "The grace of the Lord Jesus Christ, and the love of God, and the communion of the Holy Spirit" (2 Corinthians 13:14, ASV). In Ephesians 4:4-6 he speaks of one Lord, one Spirit, one God and Father.

2. He is clearly distinguished from the Father and the Son. The Holy Spirit must not be regarded simply as a manifestation of God, as though He does not have a separate identity. The prophet Isaiah in a prophetic passage quotes the Messiah as saying, "Now the Lord God, and His Spirit, hath sent me" (48:16). This distinction of identities is also evident at the baptism of Jesus. The Son of God was standing in the Jordan River, the Holy Spirit came upon Him in the form of a dove, and the Father spoke from heaven (Luke 3:21, 22).

In the Bible the Holy Spirit is often called the Spirit of God, or the Spirit of the Lord. Because of this, some have concluded that He does not have independent existence, and that He must be regarded simply as a manifestation of God. But such titles emphasize that this Spirit is divine and not evil. There are many evil, satanic spirits at work in our world, but only one divine, Holy Spirit. The Tripersonality of the Godhead must be maintained; otherwise, it is impossible to come to a satisfactory understanding of some passages of Scripture.

3. He has divine attributes. Divine attributes are characteristics or qualities that God alone possesses. Among the most important of these are:

Eternality. God alone has neither beginning nor ending. Hebrews 9:14 speaks thus of the Holy Spirit when it describes Him as "the eternal Spirit."

Omnipotence. The Holy Spirit is all-powerful. This is evident throughout Scripture by the mighty signs and wonders that are wrought by Him (Romans 15:19; Hebrews 2:4). He participated in the creation of our world (Genesis 1:2). He effects the new creation, or the new birth (John 3:5; Titus 3:5). He raises from the dead (Romans 1:3, 4; 8:11).

Omnipresence. He is everywhere present. David said, "Whither shall I go from thy Spirit? Or whither shall I flee from thy presence?" (Psalm 139:7). And the answer is an obvious Nowhere! Difficult as it is for the human, finite mind to comprehend, the Spirit of God is simultaneously present everywhere. How else would it be possible for Christians everywhere to be engaged in worship at the same time, inasmuch as worship is possible only by means of the Holy Spirit (John 4:23, 24; Philippians 3:3)?

Omniscience. The Holy Spirit is all-knowing. There is nothing that is hidden from Him (1 Corinthians 2:10, 11). As the One who inspired Holy Scripture, He revealed to Moses details of the creation story that would be otherwise unknowable to man. By the operation of gifts of the Spirit, such as prophecy and a word of knowledge, He discloses inner secrets and sins of men's hearts (1 Corinthians 14:24, 25). He guides God's people into all truth (John 16:13) and gives them spiritual insight (1 Corinthians 2:9, 10). Not only is the Holy Spirit omniscient in matters pertaining to the eternal past and the present; He also knows all about the future. It was He who moved upon the Biblical writers to record events of the last days, for Jesus said that the Spirit would show His disciples "things to come" (John 16:13). And Paul records, "Now the Spirit speaketh expressly, that in the latter times some shall depart from the faith, giving heed to seducing spirits, and doctrines of devils" (1 Timothy 4:1).

Absolute Holiness. The designation "Holy Spirit" occurs more than 90 times in Scripture, with all but three references being in the New Testament. He is specifically called *the* Holy Spirit, indicating His unique holiness and also His separation from all other spirit-beings such as Satan, evil spirits, and angels. Paul goes so far as to call Him the Spirit of holiness (Romans 1 :4)—which is really the way the title "Holy Spirit" is expressed in the Hebrew language (Psalm 51:11; Isaiah 63:10, 11).

4. He performs the works of Deity. God alone can create and sustain our universe. He alone can regenerate and spiritually resurrects souls that are dead in trespasses and sin. He alone has power to raise from the dead. Yet, as we have previously noted, the Holy Spirit either participates in or is the sole agent of these works.

5. He is expressly called God. The apostle Peter accepted without question the full deity of the Holy Spirit. This is especially evident in the account of his encounter with Ananias and Sapphira (Acts 5:1-11). Peter said to Ananias, "Why hath Satan filled thine heart *to lie to the Holy Ghost?*" (v. 3). Then in the following verse he

says, "Thou hast not *lied* unto men, but *unto God*." When one sins against the Holy Spirit he is sinning against God.

Prayer and Praise to the Holy Spirit. Is it proper to pray to the Holy Spirit, or to ascribe praise to Him? This is a natural question to raise now that we have established both His personality and His deity. We have already seen that He is coequal with the Father and the Son. But there is no clear indication in Scripture that He may be addressed in prayer or worship. Prayer is normally made to the Father through Jesus our Mediator, and it is done in or by the Holy Spirit (John 4:23, 24; Philippians 3:3).

There are two prayers in the New Testament that indirectly invoke the Holy Spirit. At the conclusion of 2 Corinthians Paul asks that the communion or fellowship of the Holy Spirit may be with the Corinthian Christians (13:14). John, in the Book of Revelation, asks that grace and peace may come to his readers "from the seven Spirits which are before his [God's] throne" (1:4). The seven Spirits are elsewhere called the seven Spirits of God (3:1; 4:5; 5:6). We have an obvious reference to the Holy Spirit, even though the number seven may confuse some students of the Bible. The Book of Revelation contains much symbolism, and numbers in this book are often symbolic. Seven is the number of completeness; therefore "seven Spirits" refers to the Spirit of God in His fullness or complete activity. Isaiah 11:2, 3 is often taken as an explanation of this inasmuch as it contains seven small commentaries on the Holy Spirit: "And the Spirit *of the Lord* shall rest upon him [the Messiah], the spirit *of wisdom* and *understanding*, the spirit *of counsel* and *might*, the spirit *of knowledge* and *of fear of the Lord*."

In the Book of Revelation there are also the four angelic beings around the throne of God who say, "Holy, holy, holy, Lord God Almighty" (4:8). This is similar to the seraphim in vision who say to one another, "Holy, holy, holy, is the Lord of hosts" (Isaiah 6:3). Some Biblical scholars take this triple repetition of the word "holy" to be an ascription of praise to each member of the Trinity.

Yet if there is no clear example in Scripture of prayer or praise addressed to the Spirit, there is nothing that prohibits it. And it is perfectly natural for one who believes the Holy Spirit to be God to pray to Him occasionally. This is reflected especially in hymns and choruses. Not only do we sing *about* the Holy Spirit; we also sing *to* Him in hymns like "Holy Spirit, Faithful Guide," "Holy Ghost, with Light Divine," and "Breathe on Me, Breath of God" and in choruses like "Spirit of the Living God," "Sweep over My Soul."

THE CREEDS OF THE EARLY CHURCH

One Church historian has defined a creed as "a statement of faith for public use; it contains articles needful for salvation and the theological well-being of the Church." We may think of it more simply as a doctrinal statement which is drawn up containing the beliefs of the Church in order that Christians may be able to distinguish between false doctrine and true doctrine.

During the first century no formal creed was adopted by the Church. But as time went on, false teachings increasingly made their appearance. Consequently there emerged three great creeds that articulated what the Church considered to be sound doctrine. Our concern is to see what each of these said concerning the Holy Spirit.

The Apostles' Creed. Contrary to what its name suggests, this was not a creed drawn up by the apostles. The exact date for it cannot be fixed with certainty, but it very possibly emerged during the second century. It received this title because it was believed to reflect the teaching of the apostles.

There are only two references to the Spirit in this creed. In the section about Jesus Christ, it says that He "was conceived by the Holy Spirit." Following that section it simply says, "I believe . . . in the Holy Spirit." It was not until a controversy arose about the personality and deity of the Holy Spirit that we find some additional statements about Him in the next great creed.

The Nicene Creed. The Council of Nicea in A.D. 325 drew up a creed that amplified the Apostles' Creed but that added nothing concerning the Holy Spirit. In A.D. 381 the Council of Constantinople expanded this creed and, because of current controversy over the Holy Spirit, included some details about His nature and work.

The historical background is this. The heresy of Arianism denied the deity of both the Son and the Holy Spirit. Macedonius, Bishop of Constantinople from A.D. 341 to 360, was especially prominent among those denying the Spirit's deity. He taught that the Holy Spirit was inferior and subordinate to both the Father and the Son, and spoke of Him as a messenger or minister. In effect, he said that the Spirit was on the same level as angels, who are God's messengers. The Spirit was thus reduced to the status of a creature. It was generally taught by the followers of Macedonius, who were often called Macedonians or Pneumatomachians (literally, "Spirit-fighters"), that the Father created the Son and that the Son in turn created the Holy Spirit. Therefore a created being—a creature—cannot be God.

This creed, which more properly should be called the Niceno-Constantinopolitan Creed, clearly stated the personality and deity of the Spirit in the following article: "And [I believe] in the Holy Spirit, the Lord and Giver of life, who proceeds from the Father, who with the Father and the Son is worshiped and glorified together; who spoke by the prophets."

In A.D. 451, at the Council of Chalcedon, the Church in the western part of the Roman Empire adopted this creed as well.

The Athanasian Creed. The origin of this creed is unknown, but the name of the Church father Augustine is associated with it. It came into existence prior to the fifth century. It is so called because it reflects the theology of another important Church father, Athanasius. Even though not composed by him, it sets forth much of his argumentation in favor of the doctrine of the Trinity.

Listed below are some excerpts from this creed. Some of the language may seem unnecessarily repetitious to us, but in an era when the heresy of Arianism threatened to displace the doctrine of the Trinity it was necessary to be explicit.

"There is one Godhead of the Father and of the Son and of the Holy Spirit, equal in glory and coequal in majesty."

"The Father is uncreated, the Son is uncreated, the Holy Spirit is uncreated."

"The Father is unlimited, the Son is unlimited, the Holy Spirit is unlimited."

"The Father is eternal, the Son is eternal, the Holy Spirit is eternal."

"The Father is almighty, the Son is almighty, the Holy Spirit is almighty; and yet there are not three who are almighty but there is one who is almighty."

"So the Father is God, the Son is God, the Holy Spirit is God, and yet they are not three Gods but one God."

"So the Father is Lord, the Son is Lord, the Holy Spirit is Lord, and yet they are not three Lords but one Lord."

"The Holy Spirit was not made or created or begotten, but proceeds from the Father and Son."

Pertinent Principles

1. The Holy Spirit is a Person. Therefore personal help is available from a personal God by means of His Spirit.

2. The Holy Spirit has intellect and the divine attribute of omniscience. He is available to assist in the preparation of lessons.

3. He is the Paraclete. His mission is to be a helper in times of need.

4. He is omnipresent. He is with the teacher not only in the study and preparation of lessons, but also in the classroom.

2

the Spirit in the Old Testament

The Holy Spirit is not a stranger to the Old Testament. He first appears in the Book of Genesis (1:2), and then is mentioned in the last book as well (Malachi 2:15) in our English Bibles. In the Hebrew Scriptures, where the book order is different, He is mentioned in the last book as well—2 Chronicles (24:20, for example). All told, He appears in almost two-thirds of the Old Testament books. Obviously, then, His work prior to the New Testament era was most important.

In the Old Testament two things stand out in its teaching on the Holy Spirit. The first is that there is no emphasis on His personality or deity. The accent is on what He *does*, not on what He *is*. It is the work, rather than the nature, of the Spirit that we find emphasized in the Old Testament. Consequently, we may refer to Him as "God-in-action." The same is true of the New Testament, but with some important exceptions, as we have already seen.

Secondly, Old Testament pneumatology (the study of the Holy Spirit) foreshadows much of what we find in the New Testament. Indeed, it would be difficult to understand some passages in the New Testament if it were not for the light shed on them by the Old. We proceed therefore to consider some of the main teachings of the Old Testament on the Holy Spirit.

CREATION

The Spirit of God was actively involved in the creation of our world. We are told that when the earth was without form, and void, with darkness upon the face of the deep, the Spirit of God "moved upon the face of the waters" (Genesis 1:2), bringing order out of chaos. He is really presented here under the imagery of a bird, for the word "moved" might better be translated "brooded" or "hovered." The picture is that of a bird fertilizing an egg and bringing life into existence. The Holy Spirit participated with both the Father and the Son in the work of creation.

The creation of man is also associated with the Holy Spirit. God said, "Let us make man in our image" (Genesis 1: 26, 27). Then we are told that "the Lord God formed man of the dust of the ground, and breathed into his nostrils the breath of life; and man became a living soul" (Genesis 2:7). The breath of God is a figure of speech for the Holy Spirit. Even though the word "breath" in this verse is not the same as *ruach*, which is used for the Spirit of God, the idea is the same. This is evident from other verses that clearly link the activity of the Spirit with the creation of man (Job 33:4; Psalm 104:30).

Finally, the Spirit of God was not only an agent in the creation of all things (Job 26:13); He is also the sustainer of life (Job 34:14, 15). All this again brings to mind the words of the Nicene Creed, in which He is called the Lord and Giver of life.

SINFUL MEN

The Old Testament says further that the Spirit of

God will withdraw himself from man if there is persistent sin. The Holy Spirit indeed strives with sinful man (Genesis 6:3), trying to bring him to repentance. The verb translated "strive" may also be rendered "remain, dwell, or abide in." The fearsome consequences of the Flood were the result of this removal of God's Spirit from the midst of sinful men.

In 1 Samuel 16:14 we are told that "the Spirit of the Lord departed from Saul" because of his disobedience of God's command. Samson, who had had the Spirit come upon him numerous times, similarly experienced the withdrawal of God's Spirit (Judges 16:20).

David's experience is worthy of note. He prayed, "Cast me not away from thy presence; and take not thy Holy Spirit from me" (Psalm 51:11). He was fearful that because of sin with Bath-sheba he would lose the indwelling of the Holy Spirit. It is worth noting that this is the first time in the Old Testament that He is called he Holy Spirit. The emphasis is upon the adjective *holy*—the opposite of *sinful*. Once again, unconfessed and unrepented sin results in the loss of the Holy Spirit. Only when one prays for a clean heart and a right spirit can he be assured that he will not lose the presence of God.

THE NATURAL REALM

In addition to His work in creation, the Spirit also operated in the physical realm with individuals. This can be seen in a number of different ways.

Superhuman Strength. The Spirit came upon Samson in such a mighty way that he was able to tear up a lion (Judges 14:6), kill 30 men of Ashkelon (14:19), and break the ropes that bound him and slay 1,000 men with the jawbone of an ass (15:14, 15). When the Spirit came upon some others, they were imbued with unnatural boldness and were able to lead their people to victory. Here we can mention men like Othniel (Judges 3:10), Gideon (6:34), and Jephthah (11:29).

Ability in Relation to God's House. When the time came to build the tabernacle and to make the garments for the high priest, the Spirit came upon certain people to equip them for these tasks (Exodus 28:2, 3; 35:30-35). Bezaleel and Aholiab were among those chosen for these apparently "mundane," "nonspiritual" assignments. But even in these it was necessary that they be endowed with divine wisdom in order to perform these duties acceptably. Can any work connected with the house of God not be called spiritual? Shouldn't any work for God, no matter how routine, be guided by His Spirit?

The physical task of rebuilding the temple after the 70-year Babylonian captivity was overwhelming. Opposition from without and dissension within threatened to abort the project. But God's words of encouragement and assurance came to the people, saying, "Not by might, nor by power, but by my Spirit" (Zechariah 4:6). What they had not been able to do with their own physical resources, God would supply by His Spirit. The work of God could never progress simply based on human power and human strength. The power of the Spirit of the Lord was needed to give them the added physical resources necessary for the accomplishment of the task.

Physical Transportation. Miraculous transportation was provided for Elijah (1 Kings 18:12; 2 Kings 2:11). Perhaps the whirlwind that transported him to heaven is symbolic of the Holy Spirit. Even the critics (2 Kings 2:16) at least mockingly conceded the possibility of such an occurrence. It seems that Philip, in the New Testament, also experienced this phenomenon (Acts 8:39, 40).

Ezekiel had comparable experiences, but it is not

always easy to decide whether he is speaking of spiritual rapture or physical transportation (3:12-14; 8:3; 11:1, 24; 43:5). This would be akin to Paul's testimony about being "caught up to the third heaven" but not knowing whether it was "in the body" or "out of the body" (2 Corinthians 12:2).

LEADERSHIP

Spiritual tasks can be accomplished only by the power of the Holy Spirit. We have ample testimony to this in the Old Testament. A number of expressions are used for the manner in which the Spirit of God made contact with men. Following are some of the most important ones, with a few representative passages:

1. He *comes upon* individuals (Numbers 24:2; 1 Samuel 10:10). This is the most frequently occurring expression.

2. He *clothes himself with* people (Judges 6:34; 1 Chronicles 12:18; 2 Chronicles 24:20). This is not normally brought out in the translations, but the verb is different from that normally used for the Spirit coming upon individuals. It certainly suggests that He has complete control of the person.

3. He *fills* people with himself, or sometimes the expression *full of* is used (Micah 3:8; Exodus 31:3).

4. He is *in* individuals (Ezekiel 2:2) Genesis 41:38).

We have a remarkable similarity here with New Testament terminology, but it is important to note two significant differences between the Old and New Testaments:

1. In the Old Testament, the Spirit of God was experienced only by a select few. It is not until after the Day of Pentecost that He becomes the possession of all believers.

2. Generally speaking, He was not the permanent possession of these Old Testament leaders. He acted upon them only when there was a specific work to be done. In the New Testament He is the permanent possesssion of all believers (Romans 8:14-16).

Oil as a Symbol of the Holy Spirit. Old Testament leaders, especially kings and priests, were anointed with oil as a sign they had been chosen by God for their task and that He would equip them with His Spirit. This link between oil and the Spirit is clearly indicated in the anointing of David by Samuel to be king (1 Samuel 16:13; see also 10:1, 6). In the next chapter we shall have more to say about this imagery as it applies to the Lord Jesus Christ.

Moses and the 70 Elders (Numbers 11:16-29). Moses, because of advancing years and the complexity of leading God's people, was told by the Lord that the burden of the work was to be distributed among the 70 elders. The same Spirit who had been on Moses enabling him to fulfill his task would now be placed upon these men. This incident unquestionably teaches that God's work can be administered properly only by the enablement of His Spirit.

In passing, there are a few additional lessons we can draw from this account. One is that the Spirit of the Lord cannot be restricted to any one locale. Since He is omnipresent, He can move upon different people in different places at the same time. It is also noteworthy that even though the Lord himself indicated that the ceremony was to take place at the tabernacle, His appointed holy place, He nevertheless was not bound to restrict all His work to that one spot. The Spirit is not only omnipresent; He is also sovereign! Let us also note that when the Spirit of God is active, there will often be critics who insist that God's workings must conform to their own standards.

PROPHECY

When the Spirit came upon the elders and Eldad and Medad, we are told that they prophesied. This is such a common phenomenon in the Old Testament that it deserves special attention.

The Nature of Prophecy. In common usage, the word *prophecy* often means *foretelling* or *prediction.* However, this is not the primary or root meaning of the word. Prophets at times did indeed foretell certain events, but a study of the prophetic books shows that much of their writings had nothing to do with the future. They were often concerned with contemporary problems.

A prophet, by definition, is a spokesman—someone who speaks for someone else. A Biblical prophet is one who conveys God's message to men. True prophecy is always given under the inspiration of the Holy Spirit. It is never the thoughts of men given whenever man pleases. Over and over again we find the expression, "The Spirit came upon him, and he prophesied." Prophecy was therefore one of the signs in the Old Testament that the Spirit of God had come upon an individual.

The Early Period of Prophecy. The account in Numbers 11 is the first instance of prophetic utterance being linked with the Holy Spirit. We are not told what it was that these men prophesied. The important thing was that they prophesied, and this indicated to the people that they had been chosen by God as their leaders.

In 1 Samuel we come across a group of prophets who traveled together. Saul had just been chosen as king of Israel, and was told by Samuel that when he encountered these prophets the Spirit would come upon him and he too would prophesy (10:5-10). In connection with this, Saul also experienced an inner change (v. 6).

On a later occasion Saul again found himself in the company of these prophets, prophesying along with them (1 Samuel 19:20-24). In this instance, however, Saul was living in a state of disobedience. He was seeking to kill David and sent messengers to apprehend him. But the messengers met the prophets and they prophesied along with them. We need to raise the question, "How can the Spirit of God come upon people who are planning evil?" Perhaps the answer lies in the sovereignty of God. The Lord will do whatever He wishes with whomever He wishes whenever He wishes! Prophesying, we repeat, was a sign that the Spirit had come upon an individual. It was not necessarily an endorsement of that person's life. On one occasion the Lord even chose to speak through a donkey (Numbers 22:28-30)! In Saul's case, the Lord could very well have been showing him that even though he was the king of Israel he was subject to the King of the universe.

A clarifying note is in order on 1 Samuel 19:24, which reads, "And he [Saul] also stripped off his clothes, and he too prophesied before Samuel and lay down naked all that day and all that night" (NASB). The word *naked,* according to the marginal note in the New American Standard Bible, means "without outward garments." This is borne out by the following passages: Isaiah 20:2; Micah 1:8; John 27. We might also note that he was under the overpowering influence of the Spirit of God for an entire day and night. Here was a delaying tactic on the part of God. It gave David a chance to escape (20:1).

Other notable prophets during this period include Samuel, Elijah, and Elisha—each of whom played a vital role in the history of God's people.

The Later Prophets. Beginning with the eighth century B.C., we enter a period in which God spoke to His people primarily through prophets. One curious thing during the earlier period was that even though there was prophecy, we are seldom given the content of the prophecies. The emphasis was more on the *fact* that people prophesied than on *what* they prophesied.

The prophets of this later period are sometimes called the literary prophets, because much of what they prophesied was committed to writing. The Books of Isaiah through Malachi record their messages. These men all lived shortly before, during, or shortly after the captivities of God's people. Some of their messages were directed against the sins of Israel and surrounding nations, with warnings of impending doom. Others contained messages of hope for the godly who were suffering. There were some that attacked the social evils of their day. Others made remarkable predictions of the coming Messiah and the messianic age.

Ezekiel is an outstanding example of a prophet whose life and message were dominated by the Spirit of God. He states that the Spirit

entered into him (2:2; 3:24),
caused him to stand upon his feet (2:2; 3:24),
fell upon him (11:5),
lifted him up (3:12; 14),
took him away (3:14),
brought him, whether physically or spiritually, to the temple (11:1; 43:5), to Jerusalem (8:3), to Chaldea (11:24), and into a valley (37:1). He indicates that some of these experiences were like visions.

Throughout this Book of Ezekiel the prophet says, "The word of the Lord came unto me, saying..." This expression is equivalent to saying that the Spirit came upon him, spoke personally to him, and gave him a message for God's people. It is by His Spirit that the Lord communicates with His people. It is by His Spirit that His Word is transmitted, as we shall see in a later chapter.

OTHER MANIFESTATIONS

In addition to prophecy, there are a number of other gifts or manifestations that are directly attributed to the Holy Spirit. The following are some of the most prominent:

bestowal of spiritual power (Micah 3:8),

wisdom, understanding, and good judgment (Daniel 4:8, 9, 18; 5:14; Micah 3:8),

teaching ability (Exodus 35:31, 24, 35),

ability to interpret a divine message given in another language (Daniel 5:12).

We should add to these the items discussed earlier in this chapter under the headings "The Natural Realm" and "Leadership."

GOD'S PROMISES

Relatively few people experienced the indwelling and the power of the Holy Spirit in Old Testament days. But a radical change was to take place under the new covenant promised by the Lord through the prophet Ezekiel. The Lord promised that a new heart and a new spirit would be placed within His people; their hard hearts would be replaced with a "heart of flesh" (36:26). He then goes on to tell the means by which this would take place: "And I will put my Spirit within you, and cause you to walk in my statutes, and ye shall keep my judgments, and do them" (v. 27). The same wonderful promise is given through Jeremiah, even though the Spirit of God is not directly mentioned (31: 31-34). In chapter 5, "The Spirit in the Believer," we shall see in detail how this promise was fulfilled.

There are two other remarkable promises. The first is in the form of a wish by Moses on the occasion of the Spirit's coming upon those who were to help him in the leadership of Israel. When Joshua asked Moses to forbid Eldad and Medad to prophesy, Moses responded, "Would God that all the Lord's people were prophets, and that the Lord would put His Spirit upon them" (Numbers 11:29).

The second promise reinforces this prayer of Moses. It was given through the prophet Joel in these words: "And it shall come to pass afterward, that I will pour our my Spirit upon all flesh; and your sons and your daughters shall prophesy, your old men shall dream dreams, your young men shall see visions: and also upon the servants and upon the handmaids in those days will I pour out my Spirit" (Joel 2:28, 29).

Only a few people mentioned in the Old Testament were privileged to prophesy. We shall see in chapter 6 how these promises were fulfilled so that all New Testament believers have the capacity to prophesy.

THE INTERTESTAMENTAL PERIOD

What was the concept of the Holy Spirit among the Jews during the four centuries from Malachi to Matthew? Some interesting developments took place in their thinking. The writings of this period are not Holy Scripture, and consequently their teachings cannot be regarded as inspired by God. Nevertheless they do help to enlarge our thinking on the Holy Spirit.

Mainstream Judaism. The following are the main ideas concerning the Holy Spirit as they are found in the writings of the rabbis and other religious books. They are given in a work by Eduard Schweizer,[1] a contemporary New Testament scholar.

1. All the Old Testament writings are inspired by the Holy Spirit.

2. The Holy Spirit is given to those who live a life of obedience to God's will. But when a devout man sins, the Spirit leaves him.

3. All the great figures of the Old Testament period were inspired by the Holy Spirit.

4. In the age to come, the Messiah will possess the Spirit. So will all the redeemed people of that age.

5. The Spirit is thought of in personal terms and as separate from God. He is portrayed as speaking, warning, weeping, rejoicing, consoling, and so on. But we cannot go so far as to say that they thought of Him as another member of the Godhead.

The Qumran Community. This monasticlike group of Jews withdrew to the Judean desert and settled near the Dead Sea. The now famous Dead Sea Scrolls were written and preserved by these people. F.F. Bruce[2], a contemporary British New Testament scholar, has given us the following information about the Qumran community's concept of the Holy Spirit.

1. He is not regarded as a person, much less as a member of the Godhead.

2. He is called the spirit of truth, of light, and of holiness.

3. He is associated with the prophets.

---

[1] Eduard Schweizer, "Spirit of God," *Bible Key Words*, Vol. III, Part II (New York: Harper & Row, © 1960, 1961), pp.7-15.

[2] F. F. Bruce, "Holy Spirit in the Qumran Texts," *Dead Sea Scrolls Studies* (John MacDonald, ed., 1969), pp. 49-55.

4. He is the fount of knowledge.
5. He is a guide and protector.
6. He purifies from sin.
7. He is defiled when God's people sin.
8. He indwells the holy community of God's people.

Pertinent Principles

1. The Spirit at times endues God's people with super-human strength for the accomplishment of His purposes. A Christian leader, during times of weakness and stress, may rely on the Spirit for needed additional strength.

2. The Spirit of God guides with respect to "nonspiritual" matters pertaining to God's house. The Christian teacher may look to Him for direction in such "nonspiritual" matters as the physical layout of a classroom and the preparation and use of audio-visual materials.

3. The Spirit comes upon chosen leaders in various ways to enable them to do God's work. As He came upon the elders in Moses' day to anoint them for leadership, so He will come upon any person who is given a responsibility in God's work.

3

the Spirit
and the Messiah

In the Old Testament the Holy Spirit was often called the Spirit of God or the Spirit of the LORD (Jehovah). In the New Testament there are several titles that indicate an intimate connection between Him and the Lord Jesus Christ. He is called the Spirit of Jesus (Acts 16:7), the Spirit of Jesus Christ (Philippians 1:19), the Spirit of Christ (Romans 8:9), and the Spirit of God's Son (Galatians 4:6). In this chapter we shall examine this close connection between the two.

THE PROPHECIES IN ISAIAH

In addition to Old Testament promises of the Spirit for all believers, there are four predictions in Isaiah that specifically link the Holy Spirit with the Messiah's earthly ministry. By the power of the Spirit, the Messiah will possess wisdom, understanding, counseling ability, might, knowledge, and the fear of the Lord (Isaiah 11:1-4). He will thus be enabled to render righteous judgments in His dealings with people. This passage applies specifically to the millennial reign of Jesus, but it is applicable to His first-century appearance on earth.

In Isaiah 42:1-4 He is called God's servant upon whom

29

God puts His Spirit. This passage emphasizes the compassion of the Messiah toward those in distress. It is quoted by Matthew in connection with the healing of the man with the withered hand and the resultant opposition from the Pharisees (Matthew 12:17-21).

Isaiah 48:16 predicts that when the Messiah is sent to accomplish His work, both the Father and the Spirit give Him the necessary authority.

Then in the most comprehensive of these prophecies, the Messiah says: "The Spirit of the Lord God is upon me; because the Lord hath anointed me to preach good tidings unto the meek; he hath sent me to bind up the brokenhearted, to proclaim liberty to the captives, and the opening of the prison to them that are bound; to proclaim the acceptable year of the Lord..." (Isaiah 61:1, 2). At the outset of His ministry, Jesus read this passage at a synagogue service in Nazareth and then declared, "This day is this Scripture fulfilled in your ears" (Luke 4:16-22).

The Earthly Jesus

The Holy Spirit was mightily at work in the Lord Jesus Christ from the time of His conception in the womb of Mary to His resurrection from the dead. During the years of His sojourn on earth, Jesus was both fully God and fully man. In this section of the chapter we shall look at Jesus as a man.

His Virginal Conception. We often refer to this event as the Virgin Birth, but our purpose here is to emphasize the activity of the Holy Spirit upon Mary at the time she conceived the Messiah. The angel said to her, "The Holy Ghost shall come upon thee, and the power of the Highest shall overshadow thee: therefore also that holy thing which shall be born of thee shall be called the

Son of God" (Luke 1:35). Matthew states that Mary "was found with child of the Holy Ghost" (1:18) and tells us further that the angel of the Lord assured Joseph that that which Mary had conceived was "of the Holy Ghost" (1:20).

The Holy Spirit was at work in the man Jesus from the moment He was conceived. He had no human father, which was a fulfillment of the prophecy given by Isaiah that "a virgin shall conceive, and bear a son" (7:14). This miraculous event, according to the prophecy, was a sign the Lord would give to His people.

His Baptism. Jesus was anointed by the Holy Spirit at the time of His baptism by John. The Spirit descended on Him in the bodily form of a dove (Luke 3:22). This immediately reminds us of the activity of the Spirit in creation (Genesis 1:2), where He is likened to a bird. There is added significance in likening the Holy Spirit to a dove. The dove was a symbol of innocence and harmlessness (Matthew 10:16); this would be most appropriate on the occasion of Jesus' baptism inasmuch as John the Baptist referred to Him twice as the Lamb of God (John 1:29, 36). The sinless, spotless Lamb was visited by the innocent, harmless Dove! We might also note that the dove was a sacrificial bird (Genesis 15:9; Leviticus 1:14), and that this, too, would be appropriate in linking it with another sacrificial animal—a lamb.

As we saw in the preceding chapter, anointing was a common practice among the Jews. It marked the beginning of a person's service to God. It indicated that God had set him aside for a special work and would provide the necessary power to fulfill his mission. Jesus is here at the outset of His public ministry, and His Father indicates His approval by saying, "Thou art my beloved Son; in thee I am well pleased" (Luke 3:22).

The meaning of the title Messiah is not apparent to the average reader. It is a Hebrew word meaning "anointed one." Likewise the designation Christ is a title, more than a name, for the Son of God. It is from the Greek *Christos*, which also means "anointed one." The two titles may be used interchangeably (John 1:41). The angel had indicated that the Babe of Bethlehem was "Christ the Lord" (Luke 2:11), but it was not until His baptism that Jesus could properly be called Christ. The Spirit remained on Him (John 1:33), and furthermore He experienced the Spirit in unrestricted measure (John 3:34).

Why did the Son of God need the anointing of the Holy Spirit in order to fulfill His mission? Could He not, by His own inherent deity, perform all the works necessary to accomplish His purpose? Jesus never relinquished his deity—even when the eternal Son of God united himself with a human nature like ours. The apostle Paul helps our understanding of this problem when he says that Christ Jesus, even though "He existed in the form of God, did not regard equality with God a thing to be grasped, but emptied Himself, taking the form of a bondservant, and being made in the likeness of men" (Philippians 2:6, 7, NASB). There are differences of opinion on the specific interpretation of this passage, but the basic idea is that the Son of God willingly and deliberately chose to limit himself while here on earth. He did not cease to be God, but He elected to live as a man relying on the power of the Spirit to sustain Him and help Him in His work for God.

His Temptation in the Wilderness. Immediately following His baptism, He was led by the Spirit into the Judean wilderness (Luke 4:1; Matthew 4:1). Mark says more forcefully that the Spirit "driveth Him into the

wilderness" (1:12). Jesus was a man completely dominated and guided by the Holy Spirit—even when it meant
40 days of hunger, loneliness, and temptation! It was there
that Jesus, who went full of the Holy Spirit (Luke 4:1),
encountered the archevil spirit—Satan.

It is often emphasized, and rightly so, that our Lord
overcame Satan's temptations by quoting the Word of
God. But we must also see that this had to be done
in the power of the Spirit. Undoubtedly, the Spirit helped
Jesus to recall the appropriate Scripture passages to effectively silence the tempter. Spiritual warfare must be
fought with spiritual weapons (Ephesians 6:11-18).
Among these weapons are "the sword of the Spirit, which
is the word of God" and "praying always with all prayer
and supplication in the Spirit" (vv. 17, 18).

Christians may also be God's anointed ones (2 Corinthians 1:21, 22). John, in his First Epistle, emphasizes
that Christians who have an anointing, or unction, from
God will be able to combat erroneous teaching because
the Spirit himself will enlighten their understanding. He
says, "The same anointing teacheth you of all things,
and is truth, and is no lie" (1 John 2:20, 27).

As in the case of Jesus, God by His Spirit may lead
us into a time of severe testing. But like Jesus, we can
emerge triumphant by relying for help on His Spirit and
His Word.

His Mighty Works. The Gospels record a succession of
miracles performed by Jesus—healings, demon expulsions,
raisings from the dead. While the Gospel writers do not
always attribute these works directly to the power of
the Holy Spirit, we saw in the first section of this chapter
how both the prophecies in Isaiah and Jesus himself made
general statements to that effect.

Following the wilderness temptation, Jesus "returned

in the power of the Spirit into Galilee" (Luke 4:14). He then launched out into His public ministry. Peter, in his message to the household of Cornelius, said that "God anointed Jesus of Nazareth with the Holy Ghost and with power: who went about doing good, and healing all that were oppressed of the devil; for God was with him" (Acts 10:38). One outstanding example of this ministry of deliverance from the devil is the casting out of a demon from a blind, mute man. The Pharisees insisted that Jesus performed this and similar miracles by the power of Satan, but Jesus responded that Satan does not cast out Satan. He went on to insist that He cast out demons "by the Spirit of God" (Matthew 12:22-30).

The Book of Acts records many instances of miracles wrought by the hands of the disciples. Jesus had promised, "He that believeth on me, the works that I do shall he do also; and greater works than these shall he do; because I go unto my Father" (John 14:12). Immediately after that statement he began to talk about the coming of the Holy Spirit. Just prior to His ascension to the Father He again promised, "Ye shall receive power, after that the Holy Ghost is come upon you: and ye shall be witnesses unto me" (Acts 1:8). The means by which they witnessed included the "greater works" which validated the verbal claims they made about Jesus. Hebrews 2:3, 4 clearly makes this connection between the preaching of the gospel and the accompanying manifestations of the power of God:

"How shall we escape, if we neglect so great salvation; which at the first began to be spoken by the Lord, and was confirmed unto us by them that heard him; God also bearing them witness, both with signs and wonders, and with divers miracles, and gifts of the Holy Ghost, according to his own will?"

His Death. We are told that Christ "through the eternal Spirit offered himself without spot to God" (Hebrews 9:14). It was through the power of the Holy Spirit that Jesus accomplished every phase of His ministry. Now His crowning work—His atoning death on the Cross—is also associated with the enabling power of the Spirit.

His Resurrection. The Holy Spirit participated in the stupendous miracle of the resurrection of Jesus from the dead. Paul tells us that Jesus was "declared to be the Son of God with power, according to the Spirit of holiness, by the resurrection from the dead" (Romans 1:4). The expression "Spirit of holiness" is a strict Hebrew way of saying "Holy Spirit." He again says that Jesus was "vindicated in [by] the Spirit" (1 Timothy 3:16, NASB). The claims of Jesus to be the Son of God were vindicated, or justified, by the mighty operation of the Spirit of God who raised Him from the dead. Had Jesus remained in the grave, His claims to deity would have been repudiated.

The Spirit not only quickened the lifeless body of Jesus; He also transformed it from a natural, physical body to a spiritual body (1 Corinthians 15:44, 45). It was because of this change that the risen Lord could appear to the disciples even though the doors were shut (John 20:19).

THE RISEN LORD

During His earthly life, Jesus' relation to the Holy Spirit was one of dependence upon Him. In order to fulfill His mission, Jesus needed to be anointed by the Spirit. But following His resurrection, there was a change in the roles of these two Persons of the Godhead. As the risen Lord, He is the One who sends the Spirit to His waiting disciples.

From the beginning of His public ministry, we are

made aware that such a change was to take place. At His baptism, the Spirit came upon Jesus, empowering Him for His work. The Father himself told John the Baptist that this One upon whom the Spirit descended was also the One who would baptize in the Holy Spirit (John 1:32, 33). He to whom the Spirit was sent would become the Sender of the Spirit!

The apostle John in his Gospel records the promises of Jesus to send His Spirit. Jesus said, "It is to your advantage that I go away; for if I do not go away, the Helper shall not come to you; but if I go, I will send Him to you" (16:7, NASB). The coming of the Holy Spirit on the Day of Pentecost was evidence that Jesus had indeed ascended to the Father. Peter, when defending his Lord, said of Him: "Therefore being by the right hand of God exalted, and having received of the Father the promise of the Holy Ghost, he hath shed forth this, which ye now see and hear" (Acts 2:33).

Jesus had promised to send the Paraclete (John 15:26) to be His representative here on earth. The Holy Spirit is separate from the Lord Jesus Christ but He always works together with Him. He does nothing on His own authority (John 16:13, 14). John tells of three activities of the Holy Spirit as they relate specifically to Christ:

1. He will bring to the remembrance of the disciples all things that Jesus said (14:26).

2. He will testify concerning Jesus (15:26). When Peter preached Christ before the Sanhedrin, he concluded by saying, "And we are his witnesses of these things; and so is also the Holy Ghost, whom God hath given to them that obey him" (Acts 5:32). We might state in passing that the three primary means by which the Holy Spirit bears witness to Christ are: (1) the godly lives of Christians; (2) verbal communication of the Word of God,

whether by preaching, teaching or informal conversation; (3) signs and wonders.

3. He will glorify Jesus (John 16:13, 14). In other words, He will direct attention to Jesus. The test of any true work of the Spirit is whether it draws attention to the Lord. In verse 13 the words "He shall not speak of himself" are often misunderstood to mean that the Holy Spirit will not speak *concerning* himself. This cannot be the true meaning, inasmuch as we know that the Scriptures have much to say about the Spirit—and the Scriptures were inspired by the Spirit himself (we shall discuss this further in chapter 9). The New American Standard Bible gives the correct meaning when it says, "He will not speak on His own initiative." Jesus is here talking about the *source,* not the *content,* of what the Spirit says.

There is one further matter to discuss in this section. It concerns the incident recorded in John 20:19-23, and especially the meaning of Jesus' words "Receive ye the Holy Ghost" (v. 22). What happened on this occasion? There are two basic views held by conservative Biblical scholars.

The first view holds that this is the time when the disciples were truly regenerated by the Holy Spirit. All believers, when they are saved, receive the Holy Spirit (we shall discuss this further in chapter 5). Even though these men had been following Jesus, up to this time they did not have a full, New Testament experience of salvation because Jesus had not yet died and been raised from the dead. This occasion marked their new life in Christ, which comes by the new birth (John 3:5). Jesus breathed spiritual life into them, just as God breathed physical life into the lifeless body of Adam (Genesis 2:7).

The second view teaches that this incident must be related to the outpouring of the Spirit on the Day of Pentecost seven weeks later. There are several links between the two events which suggest that what happened on Easter Sunday was a foretaste, or a reinforcement, of the promise of the Spirit that was fulfilled in Acts 2. First of all, we have a command to receive the Spirit. Unsaved people are never commanded to receive the Spirit; they are commanded to repent and believe in Jesus Christ. But the disciples *were* commanded to remain in Jerusalem until they were filled with the Spirit (Luke 24:49; Acts 1:4, 5). In the second place, we see Jesus breathing on them. This could be connected with the "rushing mighty wind" on the Day of Pentecost (Acts 2:2), since both breath and wind are air in motion. Perhaps when the disciples heard the wind they were reminded of the breath of Jesus on them and knew that the Spirit was about to come upon them.

There is one further link between the two incidents. It is always important to interpret a verse of Scripture in the light of its context. In the verse preceding Jesus' command to receive the Spirit, He says, "As my Father hath sent me, even so send I you" (John 20:21). In the verse following the command, He says, "Whosesoever sins ye remit, they are remitted unto them; and whosesoever sins ye retain, they are retained" (v. 23). We cannot take time to interpret this verse in detail, but it is clear that both verse 21 and verse 23 deal with *service* to the Lord, not *salvation*. This is what we find in Acts 1:8, where Jesus connects the baptism in the Holy Spirit with service, "But ye shall receive power, after that the Holy Ghost is come upon you: and ye shall be witnesses unto me."

It therefore seems preferable to accept the second interpretation, but each student of Scripture is free to accept the view he feels is in harmony with the rest of Scripture.

SUBORDINATION OF THE SPIRIT

From some of the statements made in Scripture about the Holy Spirit, we may receive the impression that He is not equal to the Son or the Father. We have already noted some of them made by Jesus himself, such as: "whom the Father will send in my name" (John 14:26); "whom I will send unto you from the Father, even the Spirit of truth, which proceedeth from the Father" (John 15:26); "I will send him unto you" (John 16:7); "He will not speak on His own initiative" (John 16:13, NASB.).

We must distinguish between the idea of subordination and the idea of inferiority. The Spirit is not inferior to the Father or the Son. All three are equally God; there is no difference as to their *nature*. But there are differences in their *functions*. All three work together harmoniously, but there are also separate functions which each has. The Spirit is sometimes called the Executive of the Godhead. It is through Him that God's blessings and presence are mediated to men.

Perhaps an analogy will help to clarify this point, though we must remember that an analogy cannot be applied in every particular. All men are created in the image of God. Therefore as far as their innermost nature is concerned, no man is inferior to any other man. But there are occasions when one man carries out the wishes of another man. Yet this does not make him inferior to the other man, even though he is subordinate to him for that particular assignment. So it is in the present relationship between the Spirit on the one hand and the Father and the Son on the other.

Pertinent Principles

1. Jesus in His human state needed the anointing of the Holy Spirit before He began His public ministry. How much more must a leader in the Church today be endued with power of the Spirit.

2. The Holy Spirit Jesus promised to His disciples would testify concerning Jesus and glorify Him. This is the ultimate goal of all Spirit-directed teaching.

4

the Spirit
and the Church

The Holy Spirit and the Church are inseparable. Wherever the true Church is, there we also find the Holy Spirit at work. In its fullest sense, the Church did not come into existence until the Day of Pentecost, because it was on that occasion that the Spirit came upon the body of assembled believers. The New Testament employs two figures of speech that very graphically depict this connection between the Spirit and the Church.

THE TEMPLE OF THE HOLY SPIRIT

The first figure of speech likens the Church to a building—and more specifically, a temple. As 1 Corinthians 3:16, 17 shows, the terms "temple of the Holy Spirit" and "temple of God" are used interchangeably. There are several direct references to this imagery, all found in Paul's writings.

The *New Testament Evidence*. Perhaps the most familiar of the passages is 1 Corinthians 6:19. In this verse Paul is not talking about the Church, but rather the individual Christian, when he says, "What! know ye not that your body [singular] is the temple of the Holy

41

Ghost which is in you, which ye have of God, and ye are not your own?" His appeal is to personal purity of life, as the context shows.

But there are three other passages that speak of all Christians collectively forming one temple. "Know ye not that ye [plural] are the temple [singular] of God, and that the Spirit of God dwelleth in you [plural]? If any man defile the temple of God, him shall God destroy; for the temple of God is holy, which temple ye [plural] are" (1 Corinthians 3:16, 17). The warning is directed at any individual who does harm to the Church, as the first part of the chapter shows. We should also note that in verse 9 Paul says, "Ye are God's building."

In calling God's people to be separate from all that is evil, Paul says further on, "What agreement hath the temple of God with idols? for ye [plural] are the temple of the living God; as God hath said, I will dwell in them, and walk in them" (2 Corinthians 6:16). In another passage he says that in Christ "all the building fitly framed together groweth unto a holy temple in the Lord: in whom ye also are builded together for a habitation of God through the Spirit" (Ephesians 2:21, 22).

Peter also uses the symbolism of the temple, but it is not so direct as in Paul's writings. He says, "Ye also, as lively stones, are built up a *spiritual house, a holy priesthood,* to offer up spiritual sacrifices, acceptable to God by Jesus Christ" (1 Peter 2:5).

The Old Testament Background. The Church as the temple of the Holy Spirit is the fulfillment of what God instituted in the Old Testament in both the tabernacle and the temple. When the tabernacle was first set up, we are told: "Then a cloud covered the tent of the congregation, and the glory of the Lord filled the tabernacle.

And Moses was not able to enter into the tent of the congregation, because the cloud abode thereon, and the glory of the Lord filled the tabernacle" (Exodus 40:34, 35).

Similarly, when Solomon's temple was dedicated, we are told: "And it came to pass, when the priests were come out of the holy place, that the cloud filled the house of the Lord, so that the priests could not stand to minister because of the cloud: for the glory of the Lord had filled the house of the Lord" (1 Kings 8:10, 11; see also 2 Chronicles 5:13, 14; 7:1, 2).

Even though God is everywhere present, there are times when He chooses to manifest His presence in one place in a very special way. We may refer to the tabernacle and the temple as places of the localization of God's presence. He elected to dwell there in this special manner. This particular manifestation of himself is sometimes called the Shekinah—a Hebrew word meaning "dwelling place" and which may be used as a synonym for this demonstration of God's glory.

We have already mentioned that the Holy Spirit is the means by which God makes His presence known. There are two passages in the Psalms that clearly bring this out. In Hebrew poetry the writer often states the same truth in two different ways in the same verse. We shall now see how the idea of God's presence is used interchangeably with the idea of the Holy Spirit:

"Cast me not away from thy presence;
And take not thy Holy Spirit from me."
(Psalm 51:11)

"Whither shall I go from thy Spirit?
Or whither shall I flee from thy presence?"
(Psalm 139:7)

When the Lord Jesus Christ was on earth, He was the special manifestation of God's presence to men. "And the Word was made flesh, and dwelt [Greek—tabernacled] among us, (and we beheld his glory, the glory as of the only begotten of the Father,) full of grace and truth" (John 1:14). A little later Jesus himself referred to His body as a temple (2:18-21). Jesus had come to fulfill the Law; therefore the Old Testament temple was being superseded by Him.

This brings us back to the words of Paul and Peter which we read earlier. The Church is now the true temple of God, indwelt by the Holy Spirit. God's presence is not bound to a physical building. Stephen reminded his persecutors of this when he said, "The Most High dwelleth not in temples made with hands" (Acts 7:48). Even the prophet Isaiah was given this message for God's people, centuries before the coming of Jesus (Isaiah 66:1, 2). We return then to the important thought that it is a spiritual temple which is now the special dwelling place of God—the Church.

When did this complete change take place? It was on the Day of Pentecost. Luke does not tell us where the disciples were when the Spirit was outpoured. He simply says that they were "in one place" (Acts 2:1). Many infer from what he says in 1:13 that this happened in the Upper Room. But it is also possible that they were in the temple area. Luke ends his Gospel by saying that after the disciples returned to Jerusalem following the ascension of Jesus, they "were *continually* in the temple, praising and blessing God" (24:53). We know from other passages in Acts that even after Pentecost they went to the temple to pray (2:46; 3:1). It would be very appropriate indeed if the Lord chose the site of the physical temple as the place where His spiritual temple would be fully actualized!

The Priesthood of Believers. The temple was staffed with priests, a select corps of men who represented the people before God. Much of their work involved the offering of sacrifices on behalf of the people.

One of the watchwords of the Protestant Reformation in the 16th century was "the universal priesthood of all believers." Martin Luther taught, as the Scriptures teach, that every Christian has direct access to God. There is no need for a human mediator between man and God. The Lord Jesus Christ is the only Mediator (1 Timothy 2:5). Paul tells us that through Jesus Christ both Jews and Gentiles "have access by one Spirit unto the Father" (Ephesians 2:18). This verse is especially interesting because both before and after it he is talking in terms of the temple. So the Holy Spirit establishes direct contact between God and us. And because this is a work of the Spirit, Peter can refer to all believers as "a holy priesthood" (1 Peter 2:5). He goes on in verse 9 to speak of Christians as a "royal priesthood"—a thought echoed in the Book of Revelation, where the idea of priesthood is linked with that of reigning with Christ (1:6; 5:10; 20:6).

The spiritual priesthood of the spiritual Temple must therefore offer spiritual sacrifices to God (1 Peter 2:5). Three such sacrifices are clearly mentioned in the New Testament:

1. Our Bodies. The one supreme Sacrifice was crucfied on the cross, so that God no longer wishes dead sacrifices to be offered to Him. He now seeks live sacrifices. Paul speaks of this when he says, "I urge you therefore, brethern, by the mercies of God, to present your bodies a living and holy sacrifice, acceptable to God,

which is your spiritual service of worship" (Romans 12:1, NASB). There is still truth in the statement that it may be more difficult to live for God than to die for Him!

2. Our Praise. Animal sacrifices were made daily in the temple, so that there was a continual burning of their bodies and the resultant smoke and aroma ascending to God. In this context, Christians are told to "offer the sacrifice of praise to God continually, that is, the fruit of our lips giving thanks to His name" (Hebrews 13:15).

3. Our Good Works. "And do not neglect doing good and sharing; for with such sacrifices God is pleased" (Hebrews 13:16, NASB). In his letter to the Philippians, Paul commends them for sending him things that helped to ease the hardships of prison life, referring to these things as "an odor of a sweet smell, a sacrifice acceptable, well-pleasing to God" (4:18).

A Body Animated by the Spirit

The second important figure of speech used for the Church is that of a body, and of the body of Christ in particular. Unlike the idea of the temple, it is not based on anything in the Old Testament. Furthermore, Paul is the only one who employs this analogy. It is one of the most meaningful ways of speaking about the Church. The key passages are 1 Corinthians 12, Romans 12, and Ephesians 4. Each of these links the idea of the Church as a body with the work of the Holy Spirit. Just as a human body is dependent on breath to sustain its life, so the body of Christ can exist only where there is the energizing of the Holy Spirit.

The Spirit Constitutes the Church. "For by one Spirit are we all baptized into one body" (1 Corinthians 12:13; see also Romans 12:5; 6:3; Galatians 3:27). As soon as a person is saved, he becomes a member of this body. He is saved as an individual, but he is immediately incorporated into the body of Christ by the operation of the Holy Spirit.

We must distinguish between this baptism *by* the Spirit and the baptism *in* the Spirit (our topic for chapter 6). The Holy Spirit is the agent who brings us into Christ's body, the Church. The main point of 1 Corinthians 12 is that the Holy Spirit is the active agent in all the works mentioned •by Paul. There are some who dispute the translation of verse 13 as we have it in the King James Version by maintaining that the preposition should be *in* rather than *by*. The Greek preposition used by Paul may be translated either way, but the context, as we have said, talks throughout about the activity of the Spirit. We should therefore retain the translation *by*. Who else but the Holy Spirit, who regenerates men, would make them members of the body of Christ?

He Adds to the Church. This is closely related to the preceding idea. Not only is the Spirit the inner life of the Church; He also adds new members continually to the Body. He accomplishes this by working through God's people. The apostle John records, "And the Spirit and the bride [another figure of speech for the Church] say, Come.... And whosoever will, let him take the water of life freely" (Revelation 22:17).

The Book of Acts is a continuous commentary on this point. It was only by the power of the Holy Spirit that the disciples were able to witness effectively (Acts 1:8). As a result of the Spirit-inspired preaching of Peter (2:14) his hearers were "pricked in their heart [convicted by the Holy Spirit]" (2:37), with the result that about 3,000 souls were added to the Church that day (2:41). We read further that "the Lord added to the church daily such as should be saved [Greek—the ones being saved]" (2:47). Our English translations do not usually bring out a significant point in connection with Peter's speaking. In Acts 2:4 we read that the disciples spoke in tongues "as the Spirit gave them utterance." The idea is that of speech prompted and controlled by the Holy Spirit. The same word for "gave them utterance" is found in verse 14, where our King James Version simply reads "said." This is a most important point for any effective soul winning. What we say by way of witnessing must be guided and controlled by the Holy Spirit in order for souls to be added to the Church.

This matter of human instrumentality in the further- ance of God's work cannot be too strongly emphasized. God could have ordained it otherwise. He could have sovereignly decided that men would be saved by the direct, unmediated work of the Holy Spirit. But He has chosen to use us, as we yield to the Spirit, to be instrumental in adding other members to the body of Christ.

Just as the Lord Jesus Christ needed a physical body in order to fulifll God's redemptive plan for mankind, so now the implementation of that plan takes place through His spiritual body—the Church.

He Unites the Body. The Holy Spirit is the only true agent in achieving genuine unity among Christians. Paul tells the Christians at Ephesus that they are to endeavor "to keep the unity of the Spirit in the bond of peace." Then he adds the significant statements, "There is one body, and one Spirit" (Ephesians 4:3, 4). The congrega- tion at Corinth was guilty of fragmenting itself. There existed in that local congregation several competing ele- ments, each claiming allegiance to a specific individual. Paul is compelled to ask them, "Is Christ divided?" (1

Corinthians 1:12, 13). Because of this divisive spirit in the congregation, he tells them that they are carnal (3:1-4). Anything that is opposed to the work of the Spirit is carnal; that is, Christians who do not permit the Spirit of God to control them in their relationships with other Christians are dominated by their lower, unsanctified nature—which the Scriptures often call "the flesh."

We must emphasize the fact that all who have been born again by the Spirit are members of the one Body, even though this may not always be outwardly evident. God's Word appeals to Christians to demonstrate among themselves and to the world that this unity is indeed a reality. This is achieved only when Christians exhibit "all humility and gentleness, with patience, showing forbearance to one another in love" (Ephesians 4:2, NASB). One of the important factors in the success of the Apostolic Church is found in the phrase "with one accord" (Acts 1:14; 2:1, 46; 4:24, 32). Without this unity among themselves, the early Christians would never have experienced the presence and power of God in their midst and in their witnessing.

He Appoints Members of the Body for Specific Functions. The entire 12th chapter of 1 Corinthians is a commentary on this. We shall look at some of the important lessons to be drawn from it.

1. There is wide diversity in the gifts and functions which the Spirit assigns to individual members. There are the operations that we often call the gifts of the Spirit, ranging from a word of wisdom to the interpretation of tongues (vv. 8-10). Also included as gifts are offices associated with the ministry—apostles, prophets, evangelists, pastors, teachers (vv. 28-30; Ephesians 4:8, 10-12). In Romans, Paul adds others that are not usually regarded as gifts, such as service, exhortation, liberality, merciful-

ness (12:7, 8, NASB). We shall study the gifts of the Spirit in detail in chapter 7.

2. All members of the Body possess some gift. "The manifestation of the Spirit is given to every man" (12:7). No Christian can say that he does not have a function in the body of Christ. Just as every member of our physical bodies has an appointed task, so every member of Christ's body contributes some vital function for the well-being of the Body. It serves no useful purpose for one person to "wish" he had someone else's gift or talent. He must determine for himself, prayerfully, what function the Lord wants him to serve in the Body.

3. The Spirit distributes the gifts sovereignly, "dividing to every man severally as he will" (v. 11). Paul says further, "Now God hath set the members every one of them in the body, as it hath pleased him" (v. 18). He repeats the same idea when he says in Romans that we have "gifts differing according to the grace that is given to us" (12:6). At first this appears to contradict what Paul says elsewhere: "Covet earnestly the best gifts" (1 Corinthians 12:31); "desire spiritual gifts" (14:1); "covet to prophesy" (14:39). But there is really no conflict between the idea of the sovereign distribution of gifts by the Spirit and the idea of coveting the gifts. A Christian must place himself in a position to be used by the Holy Spirit and to receive spiritual gifts, but the actual bestowal of the gifts is the prerogative of the Spirit. God in His wisdom—and for reasons not always communicated to us—grants gifts to others that we ourselves might like to manifest.

4. There is interdependence among all the members of the Body. "The eye cannot say unto the hand, I have no need of thee: nor again the head to the feet, I have no need of you" (1 Corinthians 12:21). No member may

consider itself superior to other members. There are two main reasons for this: (1) Such a "superior" member cannot exist in isolation from the other members—even the "inferior" members—any more than one's "superior" head can exist apart from his "inferior" hands which supply food for his "inferior" stomach which provides nourishment for the entire body, including the head. (2) The gifts are not distributed on the basis of personal merit; they are distributed sovereignly by God. This immediately rules out any possibility of boasting.

5. All the members share in the joys or sorrows of any one member. "Whether one member suffer, all the members suffer with it; or one member be honored, all the members rejoice with it" (1 Corinthians 12:26). When a person's ear aches, his entire body suffers. When beautiful music falls on his ears, it is not only the ears that are delighted; the entire body enjoys it. So it is, ideally, in the body of Christ. As someone has well put it, "Our sorrows are divided and our joys are multiplied."

6. The overarching purpose of the divine bestowal of these different gifts on the members of the Body is the edification or building up of the Church. "To each one is given the manifestation of the Spirit for the common good" (1 Corinthians 12:7, NASB). The gifts, talents, and ministries that God by His Spirit grants to the members of the Body are primarily for the strengthening and edification of the Church, even though at times they serve to edify the individual himself.

THE FELLOWSHIP OF THE SPIRIT

In two passages Paul uses the expression "the fellowship of the Spirit" (2 Corinthians 13:14; Philippians 2:1). This concept is inseparable from that of the Church as the body of Christ. The Greek word for "fellowship" is *koinonia,* and may be translated as "communion," "fellowship," or "participation." There are two basic interpretations of the phrase, but they are not mutually exclusive. One view holds that it means the partaking of the Holy Spirit by Christians. The other view teaches that Paul is referring to the work of the Spirit which forms Christians into a community or a fellowship.

Both interpretations have a firm basis in what the Scriptures teach in other passages, and one is impossible without the other. It is only when we have partaken of the Holy Spirit (1 Corinthians 12:13; Hebrews 6:4) that we are privileged to enter the fellowship created by Him—the Church. This idea of the fellowship of the Spirit is not found in the Old Testament, inasmuch as only selected individuals partook of the Spirit prior to the outpouring on the Day of Pentecost.

Pertinent Principles

1. Both the individual Christian and the Church are temples of the Holy Spirit. The Christian leader consequently is responsible for maintaining personal purity of life and helping those in his charge to achieve the same spiritual goal.

2. All Christians are integrally related to one another as a result of having been baptized by the Spirit into the body of Christ. Not only does the student need the teacher; the alert teacher is constantly challenged by the contributions his students make to his own life.

3. The Spirit is the one who adds to the Church. Almost always this is accomplished through human instrumentality. The Spirit-guided teacher is in an optimum position to lead students to a saving knowledge of the Lord Jesus Christ.

5

the Holy Spirit
in the believer

Jesus in His earthly state was a man completely controlled by the Holy Spirit. Fom the time of His miraculous conception in the womb of Mary to His resurrection from the dead and exaltation at the right hand of the Father, the Spirit of God was mightily at work in Him. So it ought to be with each Christian, for from beginning to end the Christian life is possible only by the power of the indwelling Holy Spirit. In this chapter we shall trace the activity of the Spirit in a believer's experience from the time of his miraculous new birth to his resurrection from the dead.

The Spirit and the Sinner

Unsaved men are spiritually dead in their trespasses and sins (Ephesians 2:1) and consequently are insensitive to spiritual things. It is only when the Holy Spirit moves upon them that they become aware of their spiritual need. They then must decide whether to continue in their sinful state or to respond positively to the voice of the Spirit. Stephen charged his persecutors with always resisting the Holy Spirit (Acts 7:51). This is contrary to

53

the doctrine of "irresistible grace," which teaches that once the Spirit moves upon a sinner convicting him of sin he will invariably turn to the Lord.

The Conviction of the Spirit. Jesus told His disciples that when the Holy Spirit came, He would "reprove the world of sin, and of righteousness, and of judgment" (John 16:8). The word "reprove" might better be translated "convince." It is He who convinces sinful men of their spiritual need. Mere logic or rhetoric cannot persuade the sinner of this need. The basic sin of mankind is the rejection of Jesus Christ (v. 9); this rejection is due to a failure to admit their sinful state and to believe in Him who alone can effect the needed change.

The Spirit will further convince men of righteousness (v. 10). This is related to the resurrection and ascension of Jesus to the Father. These events demonstrated that He was indeed the Son of God (Romans 1:4) and that His claims were righteous or justified. This concept of righteousness also involves the idea of the "rightness" of God in punishing unrepentant sinners (Romans 1:18). But it also includes the justification of the sinner—his "right-standing" before God when he repents and believes (Romans 4:25).

Finally, the Spirit will convince of judgment (John 16:11). The prince of this world, Satan, suffered a series of crushing defeats at the hands of Jesus which culminated in His resurrection from the dead. He has already been judged, and every sinner who truly believes in Jesus Christ serves as a continuing evidence of this defeat of Satan!

The Means of Conviction. Conviction of sin comes only by the Holy Spirit. But only in very rare instances does He bypass human instrumentality in speaking to the hearts of sinful men. The means He employs is the message of the gospel delivered by faithful witnesses. Paul, in Romans 10:9-17, stresses the need for those who will share the message of salvation with others.

Throughout the Book of Acts we have a record of the message of the Early Church. It consisted basically of the message of Jesus Christ as the Saviour and the need to believe in Him on the basis of His death and resurrection, lest the judgment of God come upon the hearers if they reject Him. The result of this kind of Spirit-anointed witnessing was that people "were pricked in their heart" and asked "What shall we do?" (Acts 2:37).

It cannot be too strongly emphasized that the Holy Spirit must convict and convince men of their need of salvation. Our responsibility is to declare and share this message of salvation, and to leave the results in the Lord's hands as He speaks to hearts by His Spirit. The apostle Paul's words are so appropriate on this point that we will quote them at length:

"And I, brethern, when I came to you, came not with excellency of speech or of wisdom, declaring unto you the testimony of God.

"For I determined not to know any thing among you, save Jesus Christ, and him crucified.

"And I was with you in weakness, and in fear, and in much trembling.

"And my speech and my preaching was not with enticing words of man's wisdom, but in demonstration of the Spirit and of power:

"That your faith should not stand in the wisdom of men, but in the power of God" (1 Corinthians 2:1-5).

On occasion God may choose to speak to a sinner's heart by the manifestation of some gift of the Spirit. This would be especially true of a prophetic utterance.

Paul tells us that through prophecy a sinner may be convinced and judged by all and "thus are the secrets of his heart made manifest; and so falling down on his face he will worship God, and report that God is in you of a truth" (1 Corinthians 14:24, 25).

REGENERATION

Terminology Used. The work of salvation is so grand that the writers of the New Testament, under the inspiration of the Holy Spirit, speak of it in a number of different ways. Each presents a special facet of the overall work of redemption in our lives. A number of these are specifically related to the work of the Spirit.

1. *Regeneration.* Jesus told Nicodemus, "Except a man be born of water and of the Spirit, he cannot enter into the kingdom of God. That which is born of the flesh is flesh; and that which is born of the Spirit is spirit" (John 3:5, 6). Peter tells us that we are partakers of the divine nature (2 Peter 1:4) and in Hebrews we are told that we are partakers of the Holy Spirit (6:4).

We can see an analogy with the birth of Jesus. He was conceived by the Holy Spirit. It was a miraculous work. It was impossible for such a thing to happen by human efforts. So it is with the new birth. It can be explained only in terms of a miracle. It is a mystery that can be experienced but the precise manner in which it takes place defies explanation. Jesus indicated this when He said, "The wind bloweth where it listeth, and thou hearest the sound thereof, but canst not tell whence it cometh, and whither it goeth: so is every one that is born of the Spirit" (John 3:8).

Paul speaks of the "washing of regeneration, and renewing of the Holy Ghost" (Titus 3:5). This is parallel to Jesus' statement about being born of water and the

Spirit (John 3:5). There are a number of interpretations concerning what Jesus meant by "water." But it is very possible that He uses water as a symbol for the Holy Spirit, just as He did when speaking of rivers of living water (John 7:37-39). The word *and* in the phrase "water and the Spirit" can also be translated "even, namely, that is," so that Jesus could be saying, "Except a man be born of water—that is, the Spirit—he cannot enter into the kingdom of God."

2. *Spiritual Resurrection and New Creation.* These are very closely related to regeneration. All three emphasize the idea of new life. We have already seen the Holy Spirit in His work of creation and the raising of Jesus from the dead. The sinner is spiritually dead and needs to be spiritually resurrected (Ephesians 2:1, 2; Colossians 3:1, 2). Viewed from another angle, he must be created anew (2 Corinthians 5:17; Galatians 6:15).

Along the same lines, we are told that the unregenerate have been spiritually blinded by Satan but that "God, who commanded the light to shine out of darkness, hath shined in our hearts, to give the light of the knowledge of the glory of God in the face of Jesus Christ" (2 Corinthians 4:3-6). When Jesus said, "Except a man be born again, he cannot see the kingdom of God" (John 3:5), He was talking about spiritual insight. An unregenerate person cannot perceive spiritual things (1 Corinthians 2:14). Such insight is available only to the regenerated person (1 Corinthians 2:9-11).

3. *Adoption.* Viewed from another perspective, Christians have been adopted into God's family through the working of the Holy Spirit. We have received the "Spirit of adoption, whereby we cry, Abba, Father" (Romans 8:15; see also Galatians 4:6). Adoption in New Testament times meant basically what it does today. It entitled

the adopted child to all the privileges of the parents' natural child. So it is with Christians. They were once children of Satan (John 8:44; Ephesians 2:2) but they have now been adopted by God.

The Indwelling of the Holy Spirit. All Christians are indwelt by the Holy Spirit. "If any man have not the Spirit of Christ, he is none of his" (Romans 8:9). The Spirit of God enters a person's heart at the time of repentance and faith and regenerates him. He remains with the child of God as long as he walks in obedience to God's will. He is ever-present to guide and assist those who have committed themselves to the Lord.

This indwelling of the Spirit must be distinguished from the infilling of the Spirit (our topic for chapter 6). The Holy Spirit is necessary for fellowship with God and worship (John 4:23, 24; Philippians 3:3). In addition, it is He who sustains the born-again Christian day-by-day inasmuch as He is the source of his spiritual life. This indwelling of the Spirit was foretold through the prophet Ezekiel. The new heart and the new spirit promised to the redeemed are followed by the promise, "I will put my Spirit within you, and cause you to walk in my statutes, and ye shall keep my judgments, and do them" (Ezekiel 36:25-27).

There is further indication of this wonderful truth when we look again at the imagery of the temple. We already saw in chapter 4 that the Church is spoken of as the temple of the Holy Spirit. But Paul also says that each of us is a temple of the Spirit (1 Corinthians 6:19). We are to glorify God in our bodies, inasmuch as they are indwelt by the Spirit.

The Witness of the Spirit. How can a person know that he has been truly born again? One very obvious way is that he has experienced a spiritual change. Once he has repented of his sins and believed in Christ as his Saviour (Acts 20:21), the old things will pass away and he will be a new creature in Christ (2 Corinthians 5:17). But there may be times when even such a person will experience uncertainty concerning his relationship with God. Ultimately, such a person must rest upon the promises of God—that if he has truly met God's conditions, then he is saved whether or not there is any accompanying "feeling" or emotion of being saved.

Yet there is an additional provision that God has made. "The Spirit Himself bears witness with our spirit that we are children of God" (Romans 8:16, NASB; see also 1 John 3:24). There is an internal witness available to all Christians which gives them the assurance that they are indeed children of God. In some quiet, inexplicable way the Spirit of God communicates to our spirit that there is no barrier between God and us, for it is by the Spirit that we have access to the Father (Ephesians 2:18).

SANCTIFICATION

Sanctification is one of the very important works of the Holy Spirit (Romans 15:16; 1 Corinthians 6:11, 12); 2 Thessalonians 2:13, 14; 1 Peter 1:2). It is the will of God for all believers (1 Thessalonians 4:3).

Meaning of the Term. The word *sanctification* comes from the same root as the word *holy.* There are times in Scripture when the words *sanctification* and *holiness* can be used interchangeably. The basic idea of the word is that of separation. When Christians are called on to be holy (or sanctified), they are being asked to separate themselves from sin and to dedicate themselves to God. The words *dedication* or *consecration* can also be used to translate the same Greek word.

Misconceptions about Sanctification. This is such an

important doctrine that theologians and many others have written much about it. Some of their views, however, are open to question. There are three extremes which must be avoided:

1. *Legalism.* This view teaches that a person can be sanctified only if he lives in complete obedience to the Law. For such people, sancitification consists in the observance of prescribed regulations. In effect, it teaches that salvation and the retention of salvation depend on works, rather than faith. Often such teaching takes the form of extended lists of dos and don'ts. Paul dealt with this problem in his letter to the Galatian Christians. He asks, "Are ye so foolish? having begun in the Spirit, are ye now made perfect by the flesh?" (3:3). This legalistic approach fails to account for the serious words quoted by Paul from Deuteronomy 27:26, "Cursed is every one that continueth not in all things which are written in the book of the law to do them" (v. 10).

From beginning to end, the Christian life is lived by faith, not works. True faith will produce genuine Christian works (Ephesians 2:8-10), but it is wrong to hold that the performance of good works in itself guarantees salvation.

2. *Antinomianism.* This is the opposite view, teaching that it makes no difference how a person lives. It has an erroneous concept of Christian liberty. It says that because a Christian has been freed by Christ, he may do anything he pleases. But Paul counters with the statement, "Use not liberty for an occasion to the flesh, but by love serve one another" (Galatians 5:13). Once again, a person who has been truly regenerated by the Spirit of God will demonstrate love by his actions toward God and others.

3. *Perfection.* It is taught by some that a Christian

may have an experience that constitutes him sinlessly perfect. This is often called entire sanctification. It is based on the premise that sanctification must necessarily include the concept of sin. But the word itself, as we have noted, means separation. Sin is not necessarily involved, for the sinless Son of God himself made the statement, "I sanctify myself" (John 17:19). The view of sanctification that is most in accord with the whole tenor of Scripture is our next topic.

Sanctification as a Progressive Experience. One recurring designation for Christians in the New Testament is that of *saints* (literally, *holy ones.*). It is not reserved for a special category of believers; rather, every Christian is a saint! This presents no difficulty when we remember that the word could also mean "separated ones." Christians are people who are set aside for service to God.

This is why sanctification is sometimes spoken of as a past experience (1 Corinthians 6:11). It happened at the time of salvation (1 Corinthians 1:30). But there is also the aspect of continuous sanctification. We are called upon to be perfect—a word that might better be translated as "whole" or "mature." We must grow in grace (2 Peter 3:18). We are not to be satisfied with any degree of progress or level of maturity we have attained. Paul himself indicates that he is not perfect (totally mature), and that he presses on toward this goal (Philippians 3:10-14).

But this is not a "do-it-yourself" project! A person matures spiritually only as he yields increasingly to the Holy Spirit. We are to "cleanse ourselves from all filthiness of the flesh and spirit, perfecting holiness in the fear of God" (2 Corinthians 7:1), but it is only through the Spirit that we can mortify the deeds of the body (Romans 8:13).

Paul further tells us that we are to experience a continuing transformation of our mind, or attitude (Romans 12:2), and that this comes by the working of the Spirit of the Lord (2 Corinthians 3:18).

Sinless perfection is an ideal toward which all must strive with the aid of the Holy Spirit. But a Christian should not allow himself to come under condemnation for not having attained it. The important thing in one's spiritual life is *progress* toward the goal of perfection.

The Fruit of the Spirit. One of the important contrasts mentioned in Scripture is that between the flesh and the Spirit (Galatians 5:16 to 6:10). As Paul uses the term *flesh* in this passage, it means anything that militates against the Spirit of God. The works of the flesh (vv. 19-21) are the opposite of anything that the Spirit produces, such as the fruit of the Spirit (vv. 22, 23).

A Christian may honestly and legitimately ask, "How can I know I am making spiritual progress? How do I know I am truly walking in the Spirit (Galatians 5:16, 25)?" One very meaningful measurement is the degree to which he manifests the fruit of the Spirit. Is his life being dominated more and more by "love, joy, peace, patience, kindness, goodness, faithfulness, gentleness, self-control"?

According to the Scriptures, the spiritual person is one who has made spiritual progress (1 Corinthians 3:1). One concrete way in which this is measured is by his willingness to help a spiritually needy fellow Christian by seeking to restore him in a spirit of meekness (Galatians 6:1)—which is one of the fruit of the Spirit. He is the person who sows to the Spirit; that is, he continually seeks to conduct himself in a manner that brings honor to God. This often takes the form of doing good to as many people as possible (Galatians 6:1-10). All this is in complete contrast to the carnal (fleshly) person who seeks only to gratify himself.

DAILY WALK

This discussion leads very naturally to the manner in which the Spirit helps the Christian in his day-by-day living.

He Is the Christian's Teacher. Jesus told His disciples that the Holy Spirit would teach them all things (John 14:26). Sometimes this is done through human instrumentality, inasmuch as the Spirit has also set teachers in the Church. But there is also the direct ministry of the Spirit as the divine teacher.

The Spirit will lead God's people into all truth (John 16:13). When the time comes for a critical decision to be made affecting doctrinal aspects of the work of God, the Spirit is there to instruct. This is illustrated in Acts 15 at the time the Early Church needed to make an important decision regarding the status of Gentiles in the Church. When the leaders of the church reached a decision, they were able to say, "It seemed good to the Holy Ghost, and to us" (Acts 15:28).

Jesus also told the disciples that the Spirit would show them things to come (John 16:13). The entire Book of Revelation is a testimony to this. In it He is called the Spirit of prophecy (19:10), and the Book was written as a result of John's being "in the Spirit" (1:10). Paul also attributes knowledge of future events to the Spirit when he says, "The Spirit speaketh expressly, that in the latter times some shall depart from the faith" (1 Timothy 4:1).

He Is the Christian's Guide. The truly spiritual person allows himself to be guided by the Spirit at all times. "For as many as are led by the Spirit of God, they are the sons of God" (Romans 8:14). At times His leading may take us into periods of severe testing. The Lord Jesus Christ, at the start of His public ministry, was led by the Spirit into the wilderness to be tempted of the Devil (Matthew 4:1). But when He so leads, we may rest assured that He is also there alongside us—our Paraclete— so that we too may return "in the power of the Spirit" (Luke 4:14).

The Spirit also guides God's people as to places of service. On one of his missionary journeys the apostle Paul wanted to preach the gospel in the province of Asia, but he was "forbidden of the Holy Ghost to preach the word in Asia" (Acts 16:6). Later, Paul was privileged to preach in that region, but it was not yet the Lord's will at the time mentioned in Acts 16. In verse 7 we are told that Paul and his party wished to go into Bithynia, "but the Spirit suffered them not." Sensitivity to the leading of the Holy Spirit was one of Paul's marks as a mature Christian.

The Spirit is present, as well, to direct the Christian in what he will say in a delicate situation. Jesus taught His disciples not to think beforehand what they would say when they were brought up before the authorities, "but whatsoever shall be given you in that hour, that speak ye: for it is not ye that speak, but the Holy Ghost" (Mark 13:11). We find this fulfilled in Peter's life when he and John had to appear before the Sanhedrin. On that occasion Peter experienced a special infilling of the Holy Spirit which enabled him to speak boldly even though he was "unlearned and ignorant" (Acts 4:8, 13).

There are additional ways in which the Spirit moves upon individuals to speak in a special way, but these will be treated in our chapter on the gifts of the Spirit.

He Is the Christian's Co-intercessor. There are times when a Christian finds it difficult to articulate his special burden in prayer. "We do not know how to pray as we should, but the Spirit Himself intercedes for us with groanings too deep for words" (Romans 8:26, NASB·). This is undoubtedly included in what is elsewhere called praying "in the Spirit" (Ephesians 6:18; Jude 20-21). And it probably includes praying in tongues (1 Corinthians 14:2, 14, 15).

GLORIFICATION

The Christian's present experience of the Holy Spirit is only a foretaste of the glory that awaits him when he finally enters the presence of the Lord. The Holy Spirit in the Christian is God's guarantee of the consummation of his redemption (Ephesians 1:13, 14; 4:30; 2 Corinthians 1:21, 22; 5:5; Romans 8:22, 23). There are several important points to notice in these passages:

The Spirit Is the "Earnest" of Our Spiritual Inheritance. This refers to a "down payment" that is made on a purchase and is the buyer's pledge that he will pay in full. It is the modern Greek word for an engagement ring—which is the suitor's pledge to marry his fiancée! Paul also refers to this idea in terms of the "firstfruits of the Spirit" (Romans 8:23).

The Christian's Body Will Be Raised by the Power of the Spirit. "He that raised up Christ from the dead shall also quicken your mortal bodies by his Spirit that dwelleth in you" (Romans 8:11). This is the meaning of the phrase "the redemption of our body" (v. 23). The same Spirit who raised the sinner from spiritual death to spiritual life will ultimately raise the mortal and corruptible body of the Christian so that it will be a "spiritual body" (1 Corinthians 15:50).

The Resurrection Body of the Christian Will Be Like That of His Lord's. When the Lord shall appear, "we shall be like him" even though "it doth not yet appear what we shall be" (1 John 3:2). The Lord himself "shall change our vile [lowly] body, that it may be fashioned like unto his glorious body" (Philippians 3:21). At that time the redemption of the Christian will be complete in all respects. Not only his spiritual nature, but also his physical nature, will be transformed by the power of the Holy Spirit!

W. H. Griffith Thomas, in *The Holy Spirit of God*, summarizes the work of the Spirit in the believer by dividing it into three periods of time: in our past or initial experience, He becomes the Spirit of sonship (Romans 8:15); in our present experience He is the Spirit of holiness (Galatians 5:22); and in the future He will be the Spirit of heirship as the earnest of our inheritance (Ephesians 1:14; Romans 8:23) and the guarantee of our resurrection (Romans 8:11).

Pertinent Principles

1. The Spirit alone convicts men of sin. The Christian leader's responsibility is the faithful proclamation and teaching of the truth of the gospel, which the Spirit will use to convict of sin.

2. The Spirit is the sanctifier of the believer. A Christian leader, above all others, must live an exemplary Christian life. There are unparalleled opportunities in the average Sunday school classroom for a manifestation of the fruit of the Spirit!

3. The Spirit aids believers in intercession. A teacher does more than teach; he is personally interested in the spiritual welfare of those in his charge, and can rely upon the Holy Spirit for specific help and guidance in praying for them.

6

the gift
of the Spirit

All believers are indwelt by the Holy Spirit. But not
all are baptized in the Holy Spirit. In this chapter we
shall explore the doctrine of the baptism in the Holy
Spirit as it is presented in Scripture. In chapter 10 we
shall discuss the doctrine and the experience from a
historical standpoint.

TERMINOLOGY USED

The Book of Acts contains more than 70 references
to the Holy Spirit. It is sometimes called The Acts of
the Holy Spirit. Therefore it is only natural that we
turn to this book more than any other for an investi-
gation of terms used for the baptism in the Holy Spirit,
for in it we have records of people actually receiving
this experience. A survey of Acts shows that the following
terms are used interchangeably:

Baptized in the Spirit (1:5; 11:16)

Spirit coming, or falling, upon (1:8; 8:16; 10:44;
11:15; 19:6)

Spirit poured out (2:17, 18; 10:45)

Promise of the Father (1:4)

Promise of the Spirit (2:33, 39)

Gift of the Spirit (2:38; 10:45; 11:17)

Gift of God (8:20)
Filled with the Spirit (2:4; 9:17)
Receiving the Spirit (8:15-20; 10:47; 19:2)

Such wide variety indicates that no one term can fully convey all that is involved in this experience. Each presents a different facet of the truth. But from the standpoint of frequency, the expression "baptized in the Holy Spirit" is used the most often when we see that it occurs also in each of the Gospels (Matthew 3:11; Mark 1:8; Luke 3:16; John 1:33). As we shall see later, the expression "filled with the Spirit" is also used frequently, but it has a wider meaning.

DIFFERENT FROM CONVERSION

The initial experience of being baptized in the Holy Spirit is distinct from the work of the Spirit in regeneration, even though at times the two experiences may occur almost simultaneously.

This distinction becomes clear when we investigate specific outpourings of the Spirit as they are recorded in Acts. In chapter 2 we read that the disciples on the Day of Pentecost were surely saved prior to the outpouring which they experienced (Luke 10:20). Under the ministry of Philip, the people of Samaria both believed and were baptized in water (8:12), but they had not yet received the fullness of the Spirit (vv. 14-17). Saul of Tarsus was converted on the Damascus road, but he was not filled with the Spirit until several days later (9:17). In chapter 19 we learn that Paul encountered some Ephesian men who are called disciples (v. 1). Throughout the Book of Acts the word disciples is applied only to Christians. Yet Paul asked them if they had received the Holy Spirit after they believed (v. 2). Then in verse 6 we are told that the Holy Spirit came upon them.

The inevitable conclusion to be drawn from all this is that there is a work of the Spirit that is available to all Christians in addition to what they experienced at the time of regeneration.

Baptism IN *the Spirit and Baptism* BY *the Spirit.* All Christians are baptized *by* the Spirit; not all are baptized *in* the Spirit. Paul tells us, "By one Spirit are we all baptized into one body" (1 Corinthians 12:13). This is the work of the Spirit at the time of salvation by which He makes us members of the body of Christ (Romans 6:3; Galatians 3:27). The Greek preposition used in 1 Corinthians 12:13 may be translated either *in* or *by,* but the entire context of that chapter is decisive in determining that *by* is correct inasmuch as it speaks throughout of the activity of the Spirit. What we see is the Holy Spirit as the active agent in the different works mentioned in the chapter.

On the other hand, in the references to the baptism *in* the Spirit given earlier, it is clearly the Lord Jesus Christ who is the active agent baptizing us in the Spirit. The analogy is between the baptism administered by John and the baptism administered by Jesus. John immersed people *in* water; Jesus immerses Christians *in* the Holy Spirit. Again, it is the context that must determine how best to translate and understand certain Greek expressions which when isolated could have more than one meaning.

To summarize then: At the time of his conversion the Holy Spirit baptizes a person into Christ; subsequent to that, there is an experience by which Christ baptizes a Christian in the Holy Spirit.

Accompanying Phenomena

The baptism in the Spirit was accompanied by the following manifestations:

Wind (Acts 2:2),
Fire (2:3),
Speaking in tongues (2:4; 10:46; 19:6),
Prophecy (19:6),
Magnification of God (10:46).

How can a person know he has received this experience? Must all the above manifestations be in evidence? Of the five listed, only one—speaking in tongues—was repeated. When we examine the instances in Acts where Luke records that believers were baptized in the Spirit, we notice he makes a strong case for tongues as an indication that one has been filled with the Spirit.

The Instances in Acts. On the Day of Pentecost the disciples "were all filled with the Holy Ghost, and began to speak with other tongues, as the Spirit gave them utterance" (2:4). Speaking in tongues (glossolalia) occurred uniformly among those disciples. From a grammatical standpoint the word *all* is the subject of the entire verse. All were filled and all spoke in tongues. There was no exception.

At Caesarea, Peter preached to the household of Cornelius the centurion. While he was speaking, the Holy Spirit came upon the hearers. The Jewish Christians who accompanied Peter were astonished that the Spirit was poured out on these Gentiles. How did they know that the Gentiles had been filled with the Spirit? The answer is clearly given, "*For* they heard them speak with tongues, and magnify God" (10:46). Glossolalia was the indisputable evidence, as Peter himself implies in 11:15, 16.

At Ephesus many years later Paul laid his hands on the band of believers, and "they spake with tongues, and prophesied" (19:6). It is not accidental that glossolalia is mentioned before prophesying.

At Samaria, something extraordinary happened when

Peter and John laid their hands on the converts. Luke does not record specifically what happened, however. Yet Simon the sorcerer desired the power Peter and John had after he "saw that through laying on of the apostles' hands the Holy Ghost was given" (8:18). There was some external, extraordinary phenomenon that arrested his attention. He had already witnessed healings in Samaria and, as a sorcerer, he was exposed to much in the magical and mystical realm. Yet here was something different. What he "saw" (the word could mean "perceived" or "witnessed") was undoubtedly the unique phenomenon of Pentecost—speaking in tongues.

Sometimes the experience of the apostle Paul is also cited, but we should notice that Luke does not record the actual infilling of the Spirit in his case. All we are given is the statement of Ananias that he was to be filled 9:17). Yet we do know from Paul's own statement that he spoke regularly in tongues (1 Corinthians 14:18), and the logical assumption is that his first experience of glossolalia occurred when he was initially filled with the Spirit.

While other external manifestations may sometimes occur at the time of the baptism in the Spirit, the cumulative evidence of Scripture is that speaking in tongues is a regular accompaniment and a necessary part of this experience.

EVIDENCES OF THE BAPTISM IN THE SPIRIT

Glossolalia. This is often called the initial, physical evidence of the baptism in the Spirit. If we choose to use this terminology, we must not understand it to mean that speaking in tongues is the *only* thing that takes place. It is the initial evidence, but there are also continuing evidences. It is the physical evidence, but there are also spiritual and practical evidences.

Power for Witnessing. Jesus promised, "Ye shall receive power, after that the Holy Ghost is come upon you: and ye shall be witnesses unto me" (Acts 1:8). Jesus had stated previously that the Holy Spirit would glorify Him. The Spirit does this by first making Jesus more real to the believer. As a result of this the believer then finds himself more eager to share his Christian witness.

The promise of Acts 1:8 is really an outline of the entire Book of Acts. From beginning to end, this book records how the disciples witnessed boldly for their Lord. As Jesus had said, this began in Jerusalem under men like Peter and Stephen (chs. 1-7). Then it extended to the province of Judea and up to Samaria (ch. 8). It reached the Gentile Cornelius (ch. 10). Finally, mostly through the missionary efforts of Paul, it extended throughout the Roman Empire (chs. 13-28).

The baptism in the Spirit is not an end in itself. It is a means to an end—the carrying of the gospel witness to the "uttermost part of the earth."

Power for Living. The infilling of the Spirit also effects a change in the individual's personal walk with Christ. This baptism takes place when one has yielded himself completely to the Lord and allows himself to be immersed in the Spirit. The work of the Spirit at that time is deepened and intensified in the life of the believer. He becomes more sensitive to the operation and moving of the Spirit.

When Jesus promised the disciples power, He meant more than power for preaching or other kinds of oral witnessing. He also had in mind the power that produces a spiritually vibrant life. Truly Spirit-filled Christians—those whose lives are controlled completely by the Spirit—will live on a higher spiritual plane than those who have not had this experience.

The fire that was present on the Day of Pentecost suggests an aspect of the baptism in the Spirit that is often overlooked. Throughout Scripture, fire is a symbol of purification and judgment, and is constantly linked with the holiness of God. The promise is that believers will be baptized in the Holy Spirit *and fire*. (Matthew 3:11). This association of fire with Pentecost is often taken to signify something like "the fire of evangelism," but such a view of fire cannot be supported by Scripture. It is more in keeping with the whole tenor of Scripture to associate it with holy living.

The infilling of the Spirit has a bearing on the doctrine of sanctification. It is not a case of "instant" and complete sanctification. Rather, it means that the *Holy Spirit* (His favorite title in the New Testament) is being allowed to work in such a way that the fruit of the Spirit become more and more evident.

How Received

A Gift. The baptism in the Spirit is often referred to as a gift. (Acts 2:38; 8:20; 10:45; 11:17) or a promise (1:4; 2:33, 39). Therefore it is not on the basis of merit. No Christian earns the right to be filled with the Spirit. He is merely expected to receive what God graciously offers Him (Acts 8:15-20; 10:47; 19:2).

Prayer. In most of the instances in Acts, prayer is in some way associated with the outpouring of the Spirit (1:14; 8:15; 9:11; 10:2, 9). Often, prayer helps to condition a person for receiving the fullness of the Spirit. Jesus promised, "If ye then, being evil, know how to give good gifts unto your children; how much more shall your heavenly Father give the Holy Spirit to them that ask him?" (Luke 11:13). Praying in an attitude of receptivity and expectancy creates the optimum spiritual atmosphere in which believers can be filled with the Spirit.

Obedience. Peter stated that God gives the Holy Spirit to those that obey Him (Acts 5:32). The only way the disciples could have received the Spirit on the Day of Pentecost was to obey the words of Jesus to remain in Jerusalem. Water baptism was specifically commanded by Jesus and the early disciples (Matthew 28:19; Acts 2:38). Since it is a command, the observance of which often preceded the outpouring of the Spirit (such as recorded in Acts 8:12, 13; 19:1-6), it may be regarded as an act of obedience on the part of the Christian. The scriptural order generally followed is: conversion, baptism in water, baptism in the Spirit. But, as happened with Cornelius, this is not an absolute requirement (Acts 10:44-48). The main point is that an obedient disposition is required of anyone who wishes to be filled with the Spirit.

Imposition of Hands. Both at Samaria (Acts 8) and at Ephesus (Acts 19), the Holy Spirit was received by means of the laying on of hands. It is incorrect to generalize and to say that this is the only way. What we do know is that God does use some people in such a ministry.

THE OLD TESTAMENT

The universal outpouring of the Spirit was specifically predicted by Joel (2:28, 29) and was the deep-seated wish of Moses (Numbers 11:29). We have already seen how varied the work of the Spirit was in the Old Testament, and have had opportunity to observe that some of His work in the New Testament was foreshadowed in the Old. We come now to the specific matter of the relation between the Day of Pentecost and the Old Testament promises.

The Outpouring on All Flesh. The prophecy of Joel

foretold that there would not be only select individuals who would receive the Spirit. He was to come upon "all flesh"—which was to include women as well as men, old as well as young, slave as well as free. Peter, in defending what had happened on the Day of Pentecost, said, "This is that which was spoken by the prophet Joel" (Acts 2:16). All believers could now experience what only a few received in Old Testament times.

On that same occasion Peter later told his Jewish audience that the promise of the gift of the Holy Spirit "is unto you, and to your children, and to all that are afar off" (vv. 38, 39). The "all-flesh" of the prophecy included Gentiles as well as Jews. The expressions "you" and "your children [descendants]" obviously refer to his hearers, the Jews. The words "afar off" were a technical description for Gentiles. Paul uses these same words in Ephesians 2:13, 17 to describe the Gentiles. The Book of Acts emphasizes this aspect of the Spirit coming upon the Gentiles first by recording the outpouring on the Samaritans (ch. 8), who were a racial mixture of Jew and Gentile; then upon Cornelius and his household (ch. 10), who were Gentiles, and finally upon the men at Ephesus (ch. 19), who also were Gentiles.

The Connection Between Tongues and Prophecy. We saw that in the Old Testament the Spirit's coming upon a person often manifested itself by the gift of prophecy. Both Joel's prophecy and Moses' prayerful wish stressed this element of prophecy. Yet we are not told that the disciples on the Day of Pentecost prophesied, even though Peter says Joel's prophecy was fulfilled. How could this be? The Scriptures indicate that there is a difference between tongues and prophecy.

The gift of prophecy may be defined as speech uttered under the direct impulse of the Holy Spirit. But we notice from Acts 2:4 that this is exactly what happened on the Day of Pentecost. The disciples spoke in tongues as the Spirit gave them utterance. What, then is the difference? Prophecy is in the language of the speaker and the hearers; speaking in tongues is in a language not learned by the speaker. Both gifts consist of speech uttered under the prompting of the Spirit. Therefore we can say that glossolalia is a specialized form of the gift of prophecy.

The Uniqueness of the New Testament Phenomenon. There is no record in the Old Testament of anyone speaking in tongues. Nor do we find any occurrence of it in the New testament prior to the Day of Pentecost. The Lord reserved this most unusual miracle for the inauguration of the new dispensation—the age of the Church!

One Baptism, Many Fillings

The baptism in the Holy Spirit is not a static experience. Nor is it a once-for-all experience. There are occasions when a Spirit-baptized believer stands in need of additional spiritual resources. In the Book of Acts there are several instances of this.

A Special Enduement for a Special Occasion. Peter received a new infilling of the Spirit when he was called on to defend the healing of the lame man in the name of Jesus. "Then Peter, filled with the Holy Ghost, said unto them..." (4:8). We are not to infer from this that he had lost the original infilling of the Spirit. The same is true of Paul when we are told he, "filled with the Holy Ghost," set his eyes on Elymas the sorcerer and pronounced judgment on him (13:9). These might be called special anointings of the Holy Spirit given to help a Christian in a difficult situation. We note also that during a time of early persecution the Christians prayed for more boldness to proclaim the message of

Christ, and Luke tells us that "the place was shaken where they were assembled together; and they were all filled with the Holy Ghost, and they spake the word of God with boldness" (4:31).

A State of Fullness. The ideal is that every Spirit-baptized Christian maintain the fullness of the Spirit as he initially experienced it. This is indicated in Scripture by the expression, "full of the Holy Spirit." It is found in 6:3 and 13:52 in a general application, and is used specifically with regard to Stephen (6:5; 7:55) and Barnabas (11:24).

Continual Renewal. Paul admonished Timothy to stir up the gift of God that was in him (2 Timothy 1:6-8). We see from the context that this refers to the power of the Holy Spirit which enables a person to witness effectively for the Lord.

In another letter Paul writes, "Be filled with the Spirit" (Ephesians 5:18). On the basis of the original language, this is better translated as "Keep on being filled" or "Continue being filled." It is possible through indifference, carelessness, or even intensive ministry for a Christian to lose or expend his spiritual resources without being aware of it. Therefore the call comes to all to maintain the steady flow of the power and working of the Spirit.

In the verses that follow this command there are a number of clear indications of evidences of such a continuous infilling of the Spirit. We will mention them briefly:

1. Spiritual joy evidenced by a song in the heart which is edifying to fellow believers as well as glorifying to God (v. 19).

2. Gratitude to God for all things always (v. 20).

3. Submission to one another, which comes from a

sense of obligation to others and a recognition of their rights (5:21 to 6:9).

Much of this is related to the topic of the fruit of the Spirit. The truly Spirit-filled person will not only speak in tongues and be an effective witness; he will also walk in the Spirit. All that he does will bring credit to his Lord.

Pertinent Principles

1. The baptism in the Spirit is available to all believers. Ideally, a Sunday school teacher ought to be filled with the Spirit. He is then in a better position to create in his students a desire for the fullness of the Spirit.

2. The baptism in the Spirit empowers for witnessing. The teacher has the privilege of sharing with his class his own experience of Christ.

3. At times God grants believers a special enduement of the Spirit to meet a specific need. During a difficult situation in a classroom, for example, the teacher may call upon God for special help and expect to receive it.

4. The Spirit-filled life is characterized by spiritual joy and continuous gratitude to God. The Sunday school teacher has a golden opportunity to manifest to his students this state of spiritual fullness both in the classroom and outside it.

7

the gifts
of the Spirit

Gifts of the Spirit must be distinguished from the gift of the Spirit. The gift of the Spirit is the Holy Spirit himself, and is another term for the baptism in the Spirit. Gifts of the Spirit are special endowments given by the Spirit to individuals in the Church.

GENERAL NATURE OF THE GIFTS

Terminology Used. The New Testament uses a number of different words to convey the idea of spiritual gifts. The general word for gift is sometimes employed, and has a meaning similar to our English word *gift*. Another term may be translated simply "spirituals," and is found in 1 Corinthians 12:1 and 14:1. It emphasizes that these gifts are the direct working of the Holy Spirit, as distinguished from other gifts. The third term is frequently used directly from the Greek—*charismata*. It points out that these gifts are bestowed on the basis of God's grace. They are freely given, and are not granted on the basis of an individual's worthiness.

Distribution of the Gifts. We are to "covet earnestly the best gifts" (1 Corinthians 12:31) and to "desire spiritual gifts" (14:1). Yet Paul also says that the gifts are sovereignly granted by the Holy Spirit, "distributing to each one individually just as He wills" (12:11, NASB). These two ideas are not opposed to each other. Christians are to cultivate an openness to the Spirit, to be used by Him in whatever way He chooses. The desire is our responsibility; the distribution, the Spirit's.

Because God delights in variety, He has ordained that spiritual gifts will be broadly distributed among the members of the body of Christ. To each of the questions asked in 1 Corinthians 12:29, 30, the answer is No. This is based on the particular way in which these questions are asked in the original Greek. We look now at the nature of each of the gifts.

Gifts for Leadership

Our starting point is the statement that Christ gave to the Church "some as apostles, and some as prophets, and some as evangelists, and some as pastors and teachers" (Ephesians 4:11, NASB).

Apostles. Jesus initially called 12 men to be His close followers. They are designated "apostles"—a word borrowed directly from the Greek *apostolos,* which means "one who is sent." These men had the responsibility of being the Lord's representatives in proclaiming the gospel.

The word *apostle* is also used in a broader sense to include men like Paul (Galatians 1:1), Barnabas (Acts 14:4, 14) and James, the Lord's brother (Galatians 1:19). There is no one definition of the word *apostle* that clearly distinguishes such a person from other ministers of the gospel. But we may state that an apostle is one who receives a direct commission from the Lord to perform a special task and who does an outstanding work for the kingdom of God. Even though the title may not be used today, it is undoubtedly true that there are those who have such a special, gifted ministry which they have received from God.

Prophets. A prophet is a spokesman, or "someone who speaks on behalf of someone else." Therefore a prophet is one who conveys God's message to men. Prophets are mentioned throughout the Old Testament and the New Testament. But in the New Testament the word is used specifically to designate those who exercise the gift of prophecy in corporate worship (1 Corinthians 14:29). The title prophet is not usually given to such individuals even though they do indeed have a prophetic ministry. In the New Testament Church, women as well as men may prophesy (Acts 21:9; 1 Corinthians 11:5).

Evangelists. Our word *evangelist* comes from the Greek stem found in the word *evangelion*—"gospel" or "good news." An evangelist is one who spreads the good news of Jesus Christ. The word *evangelist* occurs only three times in the New Testament (Ephesians 4:11; Acts 21:8; 2 Timothy 4:5). The special function of the evangelist is to reach unsaved men with the message of salvation. He is a minister of the gospel to whom this special task is delegated. Yet all Christians are called upon to share the good news of salvation. While not all are called to be evangelists, all are definitely called to evangelize!

Pastors. The Greek words for *pastor* and *shepherd* are identical. The pastor is the shepherd of God's flock and tends to the spiritual needs of his sheep (John 21:15-17; Acts 20:28). Pastors are given two other designations in the New Testament—elders and bishops. When they are called elders (or presbyters) the emphasis is upon their spiritual maturity. As bishops, they are overseers (the meaning of the Greek word *episkopoi*).

Teachers. Pastors are to be men who are "able to teach" (1 Timothy 3:2; NASB) and in many respects are teachers of the Word of God. But teachers also constitute a distinct group of leaders in the Church (Acts 13:1; 1 Corinthians 12:28). Their function is to expound the Word of God to His people so that they may be firmly grounded in the faith.

Other Leadership Gifts. Two other leadership gifts are mentioned in 1 Corinthians 12:28—helps and governments. One modern translation renders them *helpers* and *administrators.* The first very likely refers to the work of deacons, which was to help the needy of the church. The second term comes from the idea of piloting a ship, and thus acquires the idea of providing skillful and wise direction. This basic idea is found in Romans 12:8, where Paul's list of gifts includes "he who leads" (NASB). The Greek word used in Romans 12:8 occurs in 1 Thessalonians 5:12 and 1 Timothy 5:17 as well. In the latter passage it refers to the work of the elder.

GIFTS OF SERVICE

The helper, or deacon, may come under this classification. In Romans 12:7 the word "ministry" is *diakonia,* a form of the word *diakonos,* or deacon. In addition, there are at least two other gifts of service—"he that giveth" and "he that sheweth mercy" (Romans 12:8). The first has to do with sharing what one has; the second, with practicing acts of charity. Certainly both of these are incumbent upon all Christians, but there nevertheless are those who are especially blessed and gifted along these lines. Dorcas was undoubtedly one of these (Acts 9:36, 41).

GIFTS OF POWER

Paul lists three interrelated gifts of power—faith, gifts of healing, and the working of miracles (1 Corinthians 12:9, 10).

Faith. This gift must be distinguished from the general concept of faith that we find throughout the Bible. Often in Scripture, faith is set forth as a requirement for salvation (Ephesians 2:8). But the gift of faith is different from saving faith.

It must also be differentiated from the fruit of the Spirit which is often translated *faith.* The same Greek word is used, but faith as a fruit is really *faithfulness*— as some modern translations correctly render it.

The gift of faith is a special, supernatural endowment by the Holy Spirit that enables a person to believe for and to expect an extraordinary demonstration of the power of God. This is undoubtedly what is meant by the statement, "all faith, so that I could remove mountains" (1 Corinthians 13:2), for in the same context Paul speaks also of glossolalia and prophecy. The raising of people from the dead, such as Dorcas, undoubtedly was a result of the operation of the gift of faith.

We should note that the early disciples did not and could not perform miracles indiscriminately or at will. Otherwise there would not have been a sick or dead person anywhere in sight! We come again to the sovereign distribution of the gifts by the Spirit. If He feels that the occasion so warrants it, He will bestow on a receptive Christian the gift of faith.

Gifts of Healing. Literally, it should be "gifts of healings." The manifestation of this gift is so prominent in the New Testament that it is not necessary to cite examples. But we ought to note that both nouns are in the plural. The Holy Spirit cannot be circumscribed as to the manner in which people are miraculously healed. Healing may come by means of the imposition of hands or anointing with oil. It may come as the result of an authoritative word from a believing Christian. It may be instantaneous, or gradual.

Furthermore, healing is not restricted to physical ailments. Peter said that Jesus healed "all that were oppressed of the devil" (Acts 10:38). Perhaps this is why it is called gifts of *healings*. Healing by the direct power of God may be mental and emotional as well as physical. It would also include deliverance from demon-possession.

Working of Miracles. Literally—workings of miracles. Again, there is diversity within this one gift of the Spirit. It can be distinguished from the gifts of healings in that it includes unusual, supernatural demonstrations of God's power apart from those normally associated with healing. Some would include in this the raising of dead bodies. Sometimes these miracles are the reverse of healings. The summary judgment of death on Ananias and Sapphira (Acts 5:1-11) and the striking of Elymas the sorcerer blind (13:8-12) are examples of this. In the realm of nature, this gift was especially prominent in the life of Jesus. His works were performed by the power of the Spirit, so that He was able to still the tempest, change water into wine, multiply loaves and fishes, etc.

Even though these three gifts of power are not completely distinguishable from one another, we may say that the gift of faith normally is a prerequisite for the manifestation of the other two gifts.

GIFTS FOR WORSHIP

Chapter 8 will deal in detail with the gifts of tongues and prophecy in corporate worship. Our purpose in this section is to see what the New Testament says about the basic nature of these and related gifts. We will give extended treatment to the gift of tongues—not because it is the most important gift but because it is probably the most misunderstood of all the gifts.

Glossolalia. The phenomenon of speaking in tongues is expressed in a number of ways in the New Testament:

"to speak with other tongues" (Acts 2:4); "to speak with tongues" (Acts 10:46; 19:6; 1 Corinthians 12:30; 14:5, 6, 18, 23, 40); "to speak in a tongue" (1 Corinthians 14:2, 4, 5, 13); "kinds of tongues" (1 Corinthians 12:10, 28); "tongues" (1 Corinthians 13:8; 14:22); "a tongue" (1 Corinthians 14:9, 14, 19, 26); to "speak with new tongues" (Mark 16:17).

1. *Misunderstandings About the Nature of Glossolalia.* Our list is not inclusive, but it suggests some of the most common misconceptions:

(a) Glossolalia is nothing more than the utterance of meaningless sounds by an individual in a highly emotional state. But if this is true, then the Christians in the New Testament were all overemotional people.

(b) The nature of glossolalia in Acts is different from that in 1 Corinthians. In Acts it is languages, whereas in 1 Corinthians it is not. But an examination of the references given above shows that both books use exactly the same terminology at times. Furthermore, Luke and Paul were closely associated in the work of the gospel and certainly knew each other's beliefs in this matter.

2. *Glossolalia as Languages.* According to the New Testament, speaking in tongues is speaking in languages not known or understood by the speaker. It is not "ecstatic speech"—as some translations render the Greek. The basic Greek term *lalein glossais* means literally "to speak in languages." The evidence for this is very clear.

(a) Acts 2 unmistakably identifies glossolalia with human languages.

(b) In 1 Corinthians 14:21 Paul quotes from Isaiah 28:11, "With men of other tongues and other lips will I speak unto this people." The background for the Isaiah passage is the invasion of Israel by the Assyrians, whose language was unfamiliar to rebellious Israel.

(c) The word used for the gift of "interpretation" of tongues is the same basic word used almost everywhere else in the New Testament in connection with the meaning of a foreign word or language (such as Mark 15:34; John 1:38, 41).

The basic point is that the meaning is "language" not "gibberish." It is possible, however, that there is included in this gift the speaking of a spiritual, or heavenly, language. Those who hold this view appeal to the expression "the tongues of men *and of angels*" (1 Corinthians 13:1) and the statement "He that speaketh in an unknown tongue speaketh not unto men, but unto God: for no man understandeth him; howbeit in the spirit he speaketh mysteries" (1 Corinthians 14:2).

3. *Glossolalia in Prayer.* Paul speaks about praying in a tongue and praying with the spirit as though they are interchangeable (1 Corinthians 14:14, 15). He also says that when one prays in tongues he speaks mysteries (v. 2). What are these mysteries? There are three clues provided. In Acts 2:11 we are told that the glossolalic utterances consisted of "the mighty work of God"; this is similar to the comment in 10:46 that those who received the Spirit were heard to "speak with tongues, and magnify God." Two other indications are those of blessing God and giving thanks to Him (1 Corinthians 14:16, 17).

4. *Glossolalia in Song.* Speaking in tongues may also take the form of singing—singing in the Spirit (1 Corinthians 14:15). This would be a spontaneous, impromptu song in tongues under the direct inspiration of the Holy Spirit. This is undoubtedly what Paul calls elsewhere "spiritual songs" (Ephesians 5:19; Colossians 3:16).

Interpretation of Tongues. This gift, no less than glossolalia, comes by the direct operation of the Spirit of God. Under normal conditions there will be no one present who understands an utterance in tongues. In such cases God has provided this gift of interpretation. By means of it, the congregation is provided with the meaning of the utterance and will thereby be edified.

Prophecy. Prophecy is essentially a divine revelation given to a person which he in turn communicates to others. The person who prophesies is God's spokesman for that occasion. Often a prophetic utterance is given to meet an immediate need in a given situation.

Prophecy is not the same as preaching. Some Bible translations are misleading on this point in that they translate the word *prophēteuein* as "to preach." But this Greek word is completely separate from the words for preaching that are used throughout the New Testament. The New Testament writers knew these distinctions, and did not use the words *prophesy* and *preach* interchangeably. Prophecy takes place spontaneously; preaching is usually a prepared exposition of God's Word. According to Paul, all may prophesy; but not all are called to preach.

Discerning of Spirits. Literally, "discernings of spirits." This gift manifests itself in a number of ways. Its basic function is to help the Christian to distinguish between activities of the Holy Spirit and those not attributable to Him. It may be of practical help in determining whether a physical or mental affliction is the result of an organic disorder or of demonic activity. It will help in identifying false teachers.

This gift has a special application to the gift of prophecy. In the list of gifts given in 1 Corinthians 12:8-10, it follows immediately after prophecy. Therefore one of its primary functions is to enable believers to evaluate a prophetic utterance.

Specific Revelatory Gifts

A Word of Wisdom. In a difficult situation, the Holy Spirit may impress upon an individual the precise solution to the problem. This may take the form of a response to a challenge, such as Peter faced before the Sanhedrin. He spoke to them upon being filled with the Spirit (Acts 4:8), and his defense before them caused astonishment (v. 13). This is certainly what Jesus promised (Matthew 10:16-20). We should note that this gift is not a permanent endowment. The proper translation from the Greek is "*a* word of wisdom." As the need arises, the child of God may trust the Spirit to give him the necessary wisdom.

A Word of Knowledge. Again, the proper translation is "*a* word of knowledge." By means of this gift the recipient is made to know something that would otherwise be unknowable to him. One of many examples of this is Peter's knowledge that Ananias and Sapphira had withheld part of the money they had received for their property. Otherwise Peter could not possibly have accused them of lying to the Holy Spirit.

Cessation of the Gifts

The Bible teaches that the gifts of the Spirit will one day cease (1 Corinthians 13:8). There are those who teach that this took place shortly after the first century A. D. It is true that some of the more dramatic gifts of the Spirit were rarely found in the Church after a certain period of time, but it is wrong to conclude that God withdrew them.

The gifts have been placed in the Church for its edification. They are one of the means by which God strengthens His people. But the day will come when the Church will have no further need of these means of edification, because "that which is perfect" will have come (1 Corinthians 13:10). This event, as we see from the context, is the consummation of our age with the return of the Lord Jesus Christ to receive the Church to himself. At that time the Church will be perfected, and consequently the need for gifts and other means of edification will be eliminated.

Pertinent Principles

1. Teachers are among the gifts of leadership in the Church. Even though a Sunday school teacher may not be a teacher in the specialized sense of the term as used in the New Testament, he nevertheless has the sacred responsibility of sharing God's Word with God's people.

2. All Christians should be available to the Holy Spirit to be used in the manifestation of His gifts. Especially must the Pentecostal leader be sensitive to the direction of the Spirit, for occasions arise when only such a manifestation can meet the needs of God's people.

8

the Spirit
in worship

Worship may be either private or corporate, formal or informal. Every Christian has the privilege of entering the presence of God and worshiping Him privately. This type of worship is usually quite informal. In this chapter we shall look at corporate worship, however, which is normally more formal. The coming together of Christians for worship is one expression of the fellowship—the *koinonia*—which they share as a result of their joint partaking of the Holy Spirit.

INDISPENSABILITY OF THE SPIRIT

Worship is impossible without the Holy Spirit. This is a unique feature of Biblical worship. It is possible for a person to participate outwardly in all the forms of worship, such as singing, praying, and reading Scripture, without actually worshiping.

Man Was Created to Worship. This truth is not explicitly stated in Scripture, but it goes back as far as the first chapter in the Bible. Man was created in the image of God (Genesis 1:26, 27). This set him apart from everything else in creation. The concept of the image of God involves the thought that just as God is a Spirit (John 4:23, 24), so man was endowed with a unique faculty which is often called a spirit. Because of this, man by means of his spirit is able to commune with God, who is pure Spirit.

Jesus Spoke About True Worship. The woman at the well questioned Jesus about the proper location for worshiping God. Was it Jerusalem, where the Jewish temple stood, or was it in Samaria, where the Samaritans had once built a rival temple? Jesus' response included a number of important elements:

1. Physical location is unimportant. Since God is a Spirit, He is everywhere. In New Testament Christianity, no one place is holier than any other.

2. The Spirit is necessary for worship. Even though the words "in spirit and in truth" (John 4:23) include other thoughts, they teach that because God is a Spirit, He can be worshiped only by the Spirit. Paul also expresses himself along these lines. In contrasting Christianity with Judaism, he says that it is we Christians who "worship God in the spirit, and rejoice in Christ Jesus" (Philippians 3:3). Related to this are Jesus' words that the Holy Spirit will glorify Him (John 16:14). The Lord Jesus Christ is the center of worship for the Christian, and the Holy Spirit is present in worship to exalt Him.

The Early Christians Practiced True Worship. Throughout the Book of Acts we have records of the believers gathering for worship. Following the outpouring of the Spirit and the salvation of about 3,000 souls on the Day of Pentecost, Luke tells us that "they continued steadfastly in the apostles' doctrine and fellowship, and in breaking of bread, and in prayers." He goes on to say that they continued "daily with one accord

in the temple, and breaking bread from house to house"
(Acts 2:42, 46).

ELEMENTS OF NEW TESTAMENT WORSHIP

Adaptation of Synagogue Worship. There is no indication in the New Testament of the different elements
that constituted a service of worship. It seems that there
was considerable variety in the services of these Christians. But most scholars agree that the Early Church in
its worship often incorporated the basic elements of synagogue worship. These included singing of psalms and
hymns, prayer, and reading and exposition of the Scriptures.

The Unique, "Charismatic" Elements. In addition to
the usual features of a service of worship, there were
times when the Spirit manifested himself through the
gifts of the Spirit. "How is it then, brethren? when ye
come together, every one of you hath a psalm, hath a
doctrine [teaching, lesson], hath a tongue, hath a revelation, hath an interpretation" (1 Corinthians 14:26).
We find in this passage several important characteristics:

1. *Maximum Participation.* Every one can be used by
the Spirit, inasmuch as all Christians are recipients of
some gift (1 Corinthians 12:7). The exercise of these
gifts includes women as well as men, for Paul speaks
earlier about women who prophesy in the assembly
(1 Corinthians 11:5). His injunction "Let your women
keep silence in the churches" (14:34) therefore cannot
mean that women may not actively participate in a
service. He has in mind the asking of unimportant questions by women (v. 35) during a service, which would be
disruptive.

2. *Variety.* When all the various elements of worship
are listed—the "usual" along with the "unusual"—we see
that God delights in variety for His people. At appro-

priate points in the service there may be those who will share a prophecy, an utterance in tongues, an interpretation, an insight from God's Word, etc.

3. *Spontaneity.* We cannot predict what the Lord will do during a service if the worshipers are led by His Spirit. Luke tells us that as certain men in the church at Antioch were ministering to the Lord and fasting, the Holy Spirit spoke (perhaps by prophecy) telling them to commission Barnabas and Paul for the work to which God had called them (Acts 13:1, 2). Spontaneous manifestations of the gifts must never create confusion, however. All things must be done "properly and in an orderly manner" (1 Corinthians 14:40, NASB).

PURPOSE OF THE GIFTS IN WORSHIP

Public manifestations of gifts of the Spirit must always serve to edify the body of Christ; they must be "for the common good" (1 Corinthians 12:7, NASB). This theme of edification runs throughout the 14th chapter of 1 Corinthians where Paul deals in detail with the subject of the gifts in worship (vv. 3, 5, 12, 26). The Holy Spirit distributes gifts sovereignly to individuals (v. 11), but they are to be used in building up the Church. Leon Morris, in his work *Spirit of the Living God,* expresses this thought well:

God, who has called the Church into being, has equipped various members of it with the gifts needed to build it up into that maturity that He purposes for it. The gifts are not given purely for the personal enjoyment of their possessors. They are meant to be used in the service of the Church, the beloved community (p. 63).

Specific values or functions are assigned to certain gifts. It will be beneficial for us to take a closer look at the two gifts that are given extended treatment in the New Testament—glossolalia and prophecy.

VALUE AND FUNCTION OF THESE GIFTS

Glossolalia. In the context of worship, there are three specific functions that are served by glossolalia:

1. *Edification of the Speaker.* "One who speaks in a tongue edifies himself; but one who prophesies edifies the church" (1 Corinthians 14:4, NASB). Even though the speaking in tongues may not be understood by anyone present (v. 2) or by the speaker himself, it nevertheless edifies him.

2. *Edification of the Assembly.* "Greater is one who prophesies than one who speaks in tongues, unless he interprets, so that the church may receive edifying" (1 Corinthians 14:5, NASB). A public utterance in tongues must be interpreted; otherwise it leads to confusion rather than edification of the church. If no one interprets, then the one who spoke in tongues ought to ask God for the interpretation (v. 13). The same Spirit who impelled him to speak in tongues will furnish him with the interpretation.

3. *A Sign to Unbelievers.* Many of the Christians at Corinth thought that speaking in tongues was the most important mark of spirituality. It seems further that they regarded it as an infallible and necessary sign of God's presence. Yet Paul says that tongues are *not* a sign to believers, but to unbelievers (1 Corinthians 14:22). God will not always choose to manifest Himself in tongues and interpretation in a church service, but this does not mean His presence is less real than when such gifts are present. Christians who meet for worship depend for assurance of the Lord's presence not on special demonstrations of God's power and presence, but on the promise of Jesus, "For where two or three are gathered together in my name, there am I in the midst of them" (Matthew 18:20).

The best commentary on tongues as a sign to unbelievers is found in Acts 2. On that occasion the Jews who had come to Jerusalem understood the languages spoken by the disciples. This was a sign to these unbelievers, arresting their attention so that Peter was able to preach to them. But this does not mean that unbelievers will always understand the glossolalic utterances. The *fact* of speaking in tongues, rather than the *content or understanding* of the tongues, may serve as an indication that God is indeed present. This does not necessarily mean that these unbelievers will then believe. Yet we can infer from what Paul says that if they reject this sign, their culpability is increased.

Gift of Prophecy. The various functions that are served by prophecy may be outlined as follows:

1. *Basic Function.* The basic function of prophecy is the edification or building up of the Church (1 Corinthians 14:4). Therefore prophecy is primarily for believers (v. 22), although indirectly it may speak to unbelievers (vv. 24, 25).

2. *Inclusive Functions.* A prophet speaks to Christians for their edification, exhortation (encouragement), and comfort (1 Corinthians 14:3). It is important here to note two things. First, there is no indication that the gift of prophecy in corporate worship was used to predict events. Secondly, there is a positive tone in these functions. They build up, they exhort (in the sense of encouraging fellow Christians in their spiritual walk), and they comfort. We are told that Judas and Silas, who were prophets in the Early Church, "encouraged and strengthened the brethren with a lengthy message" (Acts 15:32, NASB).

3. *Teaching Function.* A prophetic utterance is sometimes used by God to instruct His people. "For ye may all prophesy one by one, that all may learn, and all

may be comforted" (1 Corinthians 14:31). Paul also says, "In the church I had rather speak five words with my understanding, that by my voice I might teach others also, than ten thousand words in an unknown tongue" (v. 19). He is here pointing up the difference between a prophetic utterance and an uninterpreted glossolalic utterance.

4. *Convicting Function.* The gift of prophecy extends to unbelievers as well (1 Corinthians 14:24, 25). A prophecy may disclose the secrets of a sinner's heart and result in his recognition that God is indeed in the midst of His people. In instances like this it is very likely that the gift of prophecy and the gift of a word of knowledge are manifested jointly.

REGULATION OF THE GIFTS

Even though spontaneity and variety ought to characterize a Spirit-directed service, there are certain limitations imposed on the public manifestation of gifts. Oscar Cullman, a contemporary New Testament scholar, says in his book *Early Christian Worship*: "It is precisely in this *harmonious combination of freedom and restriction* that there lies the greatness and uniqueness of the early Christian service of worship."

Glossolalia. The public use of tongues may be abused. Often this is because those who speak in tongues are not aware of the Biblical limitations placed upon them. In 1 Corinthians 14:27, 28 there are three restrictions placed upon the public exercise of this gift:

1. There should be a maximum of only three utterances in tongues in one service. Paul does not give the explicit reason for this limitation, but one reason certainly is that God has endowed the Church with such a rich variety of gifts that He does not want His people to become preoccupied with just one of them. As Spirit-

filled Christians become aware of the ministry of the other gifts, they will allow themselves to be used in different ways for the edification of fellow believers. We should also mention that no gift of utterance must be permitted to preempt the place and authority of the Word of God in a service. A heavy reliance on gifts of this type inevitably leads to a subordination of the Scriptures.

2. These utterances must be given one at a time. If all or several Christians were to speak out in tongues at the same time, a charge of madness may justly be brought against them (1 Corinthians 14:23).

3. Glossolalic utterances must be interpreted. We should note the following matters:

(a) There is to be only one interpretation (v. 27). It is possible that more than one person will be able to give the interpretation; in such a case confusion must be avoided by permitting only one to speak.

(b) The would-be speaker in tongues is to keep silent if there is no interpreter present. Evidently there are those who are regularly used by the Spirit to interpret such utterances. If such persons are not present and someone nevertheless speaks out in tongues, then there are two possible sources for interpretation: someone who does not usually interpret may be so used by the Spirit; or, if such does not happen, then the one who spoke in tongues is to pray for the interpretation and give it (1 Corinthians 14:5, 13).

It is evident from these regulations that speaking in tongues is controllable. The person who feels moved to speak in tongues has the ability, if the occasion so warrants, to restrain the impulse. What Paul says about prophets (1 Corinthians 14:32) is equally true of glossolalists: "The spirits of the prophets are subject to the prophets."

Glossolalia in Acts Compared with These Restrictions.
An examination of the occurrences of glossolalia in the
Book of Acts shows a violation of every one of the restrictions found in 1 Corinthians. The limitation of three
speakers in tongues is violated on the Day of Pentecost
(all spoke in tongues, 2:4), at the household of Cornelius (10:45, 46), and at Ephesus (19:1-7).

Furthermore, those who spoke in tongues in Acts did
not speak in sequence. This is especially clear in the
cases of the Jerusalem (ch. 2) and Caesarea (ch. 10)
glossolalia, and is probably true of the Ephesus glossolalia, as well (ch. 19). The phenomenon recorded in Acts
appears to have been more spontaneous than 1 Corinthians
would allow.

Finally, we should note that in none of the cases
in Acts was there an interpretation of the glossolalia.
The "devout men" in Jerusalem (2:5-8) understood what
was said, but this was not the gift of interpretation of
tongues. What they heard was simply the mighty works
of God "in our tongues" (2:11).

Luke, the writer of Acts, had been closely associated
with Paul, and certainly was aware of his teaching on
the regulation of glossolalia. Consequently we need to
ask why there is this apparent disparity between Acts and
1 Corinthians. A comparison of the two books indicates
two points of interest:

1. In Acts the speaking in tongues is more spontaneous; in 1 Corinthians it is to be restrained and regu-
lated.

2. In Acts the tongues are associated with the reception of the fullness of the Holy Spirit. In 1 Corinthians there is no teaching on glossolalia as an accompaniment of the initial experience of that fullness. In
1 Corinthians glossolalia is *one* of the gifts of the Spirit,

not an accompaniment of *the* gift of the Spirit as in Acts.

In the light of this, there is no contradiction between the two books. Speaking in tongues as recorded in Acts served a function that is not mentioned in 1 Corinthians, namely, that it accompanied the baptism in the Holy Spirit. .

Concluding Note on Glossolalia. The apostle Paul clearly restricts the public exercise of glossolalia. But he also recognizes the value of the gift and, rather than discourage its manifestation, he says, "forbid not to speak with tongues" (1 Corinthians 14:39) and "I would that ye all spake with tongues" (14:5). Not only this, but he himself claims to be the arch-glossolalist! "I thank my God, I speak with tongues more than ye all" (14:18). James Moffatt, in his commentary on First Corinthians, says that Paul

values the gift as something not only good but exalted; it is a divine manifestation of the Spirit, to be coveted (14:1-5, 39). He himself is proud of having the gift, and he never dreams of doubting the reality of an inspired ecstasy which he knew from experience to be authentic.

Gift of Prophecy. Desirable as prophetic utterances are in a service, they too come under specific regulations (1 Corinthians 14:29-33). There are three basic limitations:

1. The number of prophecies is limited to three. The reason for this is the same as for the limit imposed on the number of glossolalic utterances. Priority must be given to the written Word of God. Prophecies, no matter how valuable, can never supplant the Scriptures as God's authoritative Word. This limitation of three does not contradict Paul's statements in verse 5, "Now I wish that you all spoke in tongues, but even more that you would prophesy" (NASB) and in verse 31, "For ye all

can prophesy." It is highly desirable that all believers have or exercise the gift of prophecy, but this does not mean that they should all prophesy in one service!

2. The prophecies are to be given one by one. This, again, is to avoid confusion. If an utterance is for the benefit of all, then it must be heard by all.

3. Prophecies are to be judged, or discerned. No prophetic utterance is to be accepted as valid until it has been evaluated. There are two means by which this can be done—the gift of discerning of spirits and the Word of God.

Prophecy and Discerning of Spirits. The order in which these two gifts appear in the listing of 1 Corinthians 12:8-10 indicates a close connection between the two. One function of the gift of discernings (the Greek is plural) of spirits is in connection with prophecy. It enables one to sense whether or not a prophecy is valid. The word "spirits" includes both the Holy Spirit and demonic spirits as possible sources of these utterances. But there is a third possibility—the human spirit. It is possible for a person to give expression to his own feelings and to think sincerely that the Spirit of God is prompting him.

Prophecy and the Scriptures. In every place in the New Testament where apostles and prophets are mentioned together, they always appear in that order. The apostles were those who walked with Jesus and received teaching directly from Him. The Bible talks about the apostles' doctrine or teaching (Acts 2:42). Practically all of the New Testament was written by apostles or close associates of apostles. Their teaching was inviolable. Even that which purports to be a message from heaven cannot preempt the apostolic word, as Paul clearly says in Galatians 1:8, 9, ASV: "But though we, or an angel from heaven, should preach unto you any gospel other than that which we preached unto you, let him be anathema. As we have said before, so say I now again, If any one preacheth unto you any gospel other than that which ye received, let him be anathema."

Prophetic utterances therefore must always be judged as to their doctrinal correctness. Paul says in 1 Corinthians 12:3, "No man speaking in the Spirit of God saith, Jesus is anathema." The apostle John clearly echoes Paul's instruction when he says: "Beloved, believe not every spirit, but prove the spirits, whether they are of God; because many false prophets are gone out into the world. Hereby know ye the Spirit of God: every spirit that confesseth that Jesus Christ is come in the flesh is of God: and every spirit that confesseth not Jesus is not of God" (1 John 4:1-3, ASV).

In both of these instances, a matter of doctrine is involved. These two tests are not inclusive, however. They merely suggest that the teaching of the apostles— which has come to us in the New Testament—is the objective standard for judging prophetic utterances.

Pertinent Principles

1. God's presence is not restricted to a building specifically set aside for worship. He is also in the Sunday school classroom.

2. Genuine Christian worship is possible only because of the Holy Spirit in the midst of God's people. The Sunday school situation, no less than the church sanctuary, provides ample opportunity for guidance and instruction in worship.

9
the Spirit of Truth

Both the Holy Spirit and the Word of God have been given to individual believers and to the Church for guidance and edification. The Spirit and the Word always work harmoniously for the furtherance of God's purposes. In fact, there are times when the two terms are used almost interchangeably in the Bible. We read in some places that "the Spirit of the Lord came upon" certain people and they prophesied; in other places we read "the word of the Lord came" and the person prophesied.

The Holy Spirit and the Scriptures are always in agreement. Throughout its history, the Christian Church has suffered because of some elements that wanted to emphasize one to the virtual exclusion of the other. Where the Spirit alone is emphasized, there will often be the consequences of fanaticism and a purely subjective approach based on the individual's own feelings. Where the Bible alone is emphasized, the result will be what is often called "dead orthodoxy." There may be strict adherence to correct doctrinal belief, but no vibrant, spiritual life to accompany it.

In this chapter we shall explore the intimate relationship that exists between the Spirit and the Word, and how they complement each other.

REVELATION

Revelation is the act by which God makes himself known to men. Man, because of his fallen, sinful state, is unable to come to a knowledge of God on his own initiative. Therefore, it was necessssary for God to reveal himself (1 Corinthians 2:11).

God has revealed himself and His will to man in a number of ways. In nature there is a revelation of God (Romans 1:19-21; Psalm 19:1), even though this is not sufficient for salvation. Further, there is a revelation of God in conscience (Romans 2:14-16), since man was endowed with the ability to discriminate between good and evil. Creation and conscience belong to "general revelation." But God has also granted "special revelation"—the specific unveiling of His redemptive purpose in Jesus Christ. He chose to do this by means of His Word, the Scriptures. The divine agent in this work of revelation is the Holy Spirit, as we shall see in this next section.

INSPIRATION

Inspiration is the supernatural influence of the Holy Spirit upon the writers of Holy Scripture which enabled them to write down God's message in such a way as to preserve it from error.

Second Timothy 3:16, 17. All Scripture is "given by inspiration of God." The quoted words are just one word in the Greek (*theopneustos*), which literally means "God-breathed." The source of the Bible is God. Since the breath of God is a symbol of the Holy Spirit, Paul is here telling us that the Third Person of the Godhead was active in the transmission of the Word of God to men. In this connection we can also go to 2 Peter 1:21: "For the prophecy came not in old time by the will of man: but holy men of God spake as they were moved by the Holy Ghost." In the light of these passages, we can say that God is the *source* of Scripture, the Holy Siprit is the *agent* by whom the Bible was given, and man is the *instrument* who, under the guidance of the Spirit, wrote the Scriptures.

We should note further that *all* Scripture is God-breathed. There are no uninspired parts of Scripture; all are equally inspired. In evangelical circles this is frequently called "verbal, plenary inspiration." It is an attempt to convey the idea that the Scriptures in their entirety, as well as every word, have been written by men who were so directed in their choice of subject matter and words that the words they employed are God's own words in the style of the writer.

The Inspiration of the Old Testament. In addition to the important passages mentioned above (which apply specifically to the Old Testament), there are other statements by New Testament writers about the inspiration of the Old Testament. In the Book of Acts Peter says that the Holy Spirit prophesied in Scripture by means of the mouth of David (1:16; 4:25). In a similar way, Paul says that the Spirit spoke through Isaiah the prophet (28:25). In the epistle to the Hebrews we find references to the Old Testament expressed in terms like "The Holy Ghost saith" (3:7); "the Holy Spirit this signifying" (9:8); "the Holy Spirit also beareth witness" (10:15). Peter, in his First Epistle, says that the Old Testament prophets sought "to know what person or time the Spirit of Christ within them was indicating as He predicted the sufferings of Christ and the glories to follow" (1:10, 11, NASB). These are some of the very clear references to the active participation of the Holy Spirit in the giving of the Old Testament Scriptures.

The Inspiration of the New Testament. The New Testament bears internal witness of its own divine inspiration. Peter speaks about Paul's letters and then goes on to refer to "the rest of the Scriptures" (2 Peter 3:15, 16). There is no question in Paul's mind concerning the authority with which he wrote his letters and conveyed his message (for example, 1 Corinthians 2:13, 16; 2 Corinthians 2:17; 4:2; 1 Thessalonians 2:3, 4, 13; Galatians 1:8, 9). Furthermore, Paul quotes Luke 10:7 along with Deuteronomy 25:4 as being of equal authority.

Rene Pache, in his *The Inspiration and Authority of Scripture*, makes an interesting observation. He says that when Jesus left His apostles,

He did not fail to promise them all the supernatural help they would need for the composition of the New Testament. In the famous passages of John 14:26; 15:26, 27 and 16:12-15, the Lord specified the different parts of the New Testament.

the Gospels: "The Holy Spirit . . . shall . . . bring to your remembrance all that I said unto you";

the Acts: "He shall bear witness of me: and ye also bear witness" (cf. Acts 1:8);

the Epistles: "The Spirit of truth . . . shall guide you into all the truth: for he shall not speak from himself. . . . He shall glorify me: for he shall take of mine, and shall declare it unto you . . . He shall teach you all things";

Revelation: "He shall declare unto you the things that are to come."

The Human Role in Inspiration. The Bible did not drop from heaven in completed, written form. God chose to transmit it to men by the instrumentality of men. He delights in using human means whenever possible to accomplish His purposes! We see this same principle in effect regarding the preaching of the gospel, which He has committed to men and not to angels or other agents.

But the human instrumentality in giving us the Scriptures raises a few important questions:

1. Were the Biblical writers always aware of the meaning of what they wrote? It is not necessary to answer this question in the affirmative. Generally speaking, they understood what it was that they spoke and wrote. But there were times when they recorded messages under the direct inspiration of the Spirit without grasping the full import of a message. This would be especially true of some predictive prophecies—such as the birthplace of the Messiah (Micah 5:2).

2. Inasmuch as the human factor is involved, does this not mean that the Scritpures are subject to error? This would be true if the Scriptures were a purely human product. In statements like "the Spirit spoke by the mouth of David" we see that the Holy Spirit is really the author of Scripture. He so guided the Biblical writers in their selection of material and choice of words that they were free from recording any error.

3. Then does this not strip the Biblical writers of their free will? This would be true if the Scriptures were dictated word-for-word to them. But there is considerable variety of literary style and choice of vocabulary among the Biblical writers. This indicates that they were free to express themselves in their own distinctive style. But if at any point there was the possibility of error, the Holy Spirit was present and active to correct their thinking.

4. Why is it so important to have an errorless Bible? Pache has given a good response to this type of question:
Full inspiration is necessary because of the fall of man. Were the Bible a mixture of truth and error, we would have to try to decide by ourselves what should be acknowledged as of divine origin or rejected as containing the alloy of human error. If man has not received from on high an exact standard, how can he distinguish between what is divine and what is human?

The Old Testament writers claimed they were transmitting the very words of God. Someone has estimated there are about 4,000 times in the Old Testament when the writers say they are conveying God's message (for example, Deuteronomy 4:2; 6:1, 2, 6-9; 12:32; Psalms 19:7; 119:42, 96, 140, 142, 151, 160, 172). Throughout the Old Testament we find expressions like "thus saith the Lord" and "the word of the Lord came, saying." This indicates that since these messages came directly from God, they would be free from error.

The Lord Jesus Christ also attested to the complete accuracy and inerrancy of Scripture in such passages as Matthew 5:18, "Till heaven and earth pass, one jot or one tittle shall in no wise pass from the law, till all be fulfilled"; and John 10:35, "The scripture cannot be broken."

ILLUMINATION

Illumination must be distinguished from inspiration. Illumination is the activity of the Holy Spirit on the mind and spirit of man which enables man to understand spiritual truth. In the section on inspiration we noted that the Holy Spirit is the divine *author* and *agent* of the Scriptures. As we consider the thought of illumination, we note that He is also the *interpreter* of the Scriptures.

The Need for the Divine Interpreter. Man, apart from God's saving grace, is spiritually blind (2 Corinthians 4:4). As a result he cannot see (understand) the kingdom of God or spiritual realities (John 3:3). Only when he has been regenerated are his spiritual eyes opened to the truths of God's Word. Paul expresses this same truth when he says, "The natural man receiveth not the things of the Spirit of God: for they are foolishness unto him: neither can he know them, because they are spiritually discerned" (1 Corinthians 2:14). When a person comes to Jesus Christ in faith, then the Holy Spirit removes the veil of unbelief and lack of understanding from the heart (2 Corinthians 3:14-18). The Bible can be studied by unregenerate men in the same manner that they study other literature, but its deepest truths are available only to those who are receptive.

The Work of the Divine Interpreter. The Holy Spirit leads believers into all truth (John 16:13). The author of the Book is its best interpreter! But for the Christian, as well as the sinner, an understanding of the Scriptures comes only when there is a receptive heart. Believers who "walk after the flesh" rather than "after the Spirit" (Romans 8:4) are unable to come to a mature understanding of God's Word. They can digest only spiritual "milk," whereas God wishes them to partake of "strong meat" (Hebrews 5:11-14). As one writer has put it, "This is why our churches are often nurseries for spiritual infants rather than training grounds for full-grown men, for teachers and for soldiers of Jesus Christ."

The Divine Teacher and Human Teachers. The Holy Spirit will teach us all things (John 14:26). With this in mind, the apostle John tells us, "the anointing you received from Him abides in you, and you have no need for any one to teach you; but as His anointing teaches you about all things, and is true and is not a lie, and just as it has taught you, you abide in Him" (1 John 2:27, NASB). Therefore a Christian must approach his study of the Scripture in complete dependence on the Holy Spirit. This does not mean that serious study of the Bible is unnecessary just as long as one relies on the Spirit of God. J. I. Packer very aptly says, "The Spirit is not given to make Bible study needless, but to make it effective." All of our God-given faculties and abilities must be employed in the study of God's Word.

Total dependence on the Spirit for an understanding of the Scriptures does not preclude the ministry of God-appointed teachers. As we have already seen in a previous chapter, there is a divinely-ordained teaching ministry in the Church. Teachers are a gift of the Spirit to the Church. Consequently they are an additional source of help in coming to a fuller understanding of God's Word.

Degrees of Illumination. All parts of Scripture are equally inspired, but not all Scripture is equally illuminated to Christians. This helps to explain the various opinions and interpretations of Christians on some relatively minor point. Ideally, all spiritually-enlightened Christians should have the same interpretation of any given passage of Scripture. But it is reassuring to know that Bible-believing Christians are in agreement on the essentials of the Christian faith—such as the complete deity of the Lord Jesus Christ, His atoning death on the Cross, His resurrection and His coming again, as well as the need for repentance and faith for salvation.

Rival Views Concerning the Interpretation of Scripture. J. I. Packer, in *"Fundamentalism" and the Word of God,* lists three views that are worth noting:

1. *The Evangelical View.* This view teaches that the Scriptures are the Word which God spoke and speaks to the Church, and are the final authority for faith and life. The Holy Spirit "who was its Author is also its Witness and Expositor." The Spirit is the only infallible Interpreter of God's infallible Word.

2. *The Traditionalist View.* This maintains that the final authority for faith and life is the official teaching of the institutional Church. This authority is based on both the Bible and tradition. Sometimes this tradition takes the form of another book or books authorized by the Church. The individual believer is denied access to the Holy Spirit as the interpreter of the Word. The interpreter is the Church.

3. *The Subjectivist Position.* At times this takes the

form of mysticism; at other times it appears as rationalism. Sometimes the two are combined. Either by some vaguely defined religious feeling or by a person's own intellectual powers, one may come to a "true" understanding of the Scriptures. This approach initially rejects the Bible as the fully inspired Word of God. Consequently, the final authority becomes the individual interpreter. For all practical purposes, this view rejects the concept that the Holy Spirit is the infallible interpreter of Scripture.

PREACHING AND TEACHING THE WORD

The truths of Scripture may be proclaimed in a cold, sterile manner, or they may be proclaimed in the power of the Holy Spirit. The promise given by Jesus was that His disciples would first receive the power of the Spirit, and then they would be effective witnesses (Acts 1:8). One of the secrets of the success of the early apostolic preaching was that it was done under the inspiration of the Holy Spirit. On the Day of Pentecost, for example, we are told that Peter "lifted up his voice and *said* (Acts 2:14). The italicized word is unusual in the Greek, but it is also found in 2:4, where Luke says that the disciples spoke in tongues as the Spirit gave them "utterance."

It is this same combination of the power of the Spirit and the proclamation of the gospel that accounts for the missionary success of the apostle Paul. He says to the Thessalonian Christians, "Our gospel came not unto you in word only, but also in power, and in the Holy Ghost, and in much assurance" (1 Thessalonians 1:5). In similar language he says to the Corinthians, "My speech and my preaching was not with enticing words of man's wisdom, but in demonstration of the Spirit and of power" (1 Corinthians 2:4).

EVALUATION OF SPIRITUAL GIFTS

We noted in the preceding chapter that manifestations of the Spirit must always be subjected to the scrutiny of the Word of God. The Spirit and the Word never contradict each other. If a glossolalic or prophetic utterance is truly prompted by the Spirit, then it will be in accordance with Scripture. The Holy Spirit is the author of both the gifts and the Scriptures. He himself has placed certain limitations on spiritual gifts, as we see especially in 1 Corinthians 14.

Is it possible for the Spirit to give revelations today that go beyond the teaching of Scripture? In other words, is God still adding to His Word? Some sincere, zealous Christians place more emphasis on what they deem to be prophetic revelations than on the written Word of God. In Revelation 22:18 a very serious warning is given against adding to the words of that book. Persons guilty of such an offense will come under the severe judgment of God. It is not accidental that this warning is found in the last chapter of the last book of the Bible. The principle can certainly be extended to include additions to any portion of the Bible.

Pertinent Principles

1. The Spirit and the Word always work harmoniously for the furtherance of God's work. A Sunday school teacher is entrusted with sharing the Word of God, which is the sword of the Spirit.

2. The Spirit both inspired and interprets God's Word. The teacher may rely on the One who, according to Jesus, will teach us all things—the Holy Spirit—to open the Scriptures to him.

3. The Scriptures are God's Word to man. Therefore their teachings must be taught unapologetically and authoritatively, by the power of the Holy Spirit.

10

the Spirit
and the Pentecostals

The 20th century is experiencing an unprecedented outpouring of the Holy Spirit. It has extended to every quarter of the globe and has penetrated virtually every denomination in Christendom. It is now considered by authorities to be the "third force" in the Church—alongside the Catholic-Eastern Orthodox tradition and the classical Protestant tradition.

We customarily refer to this "third force" as the Pentecostal Movement. But even that designation has limitations inasmuch as it is generally reserved for those who have been called Pentecostals since the turn of this century. The "third force" today also includes those who are called Neo-Pentecostals and Catholic Pentecostals.

ANTECEDENTS

Modern Pentecostals cannot claim to be the only Christians who have experienced such an outpouring of the Spirit after the first century. Church history records numerous instances of individuals and groups who have had Pentecostal or charismatic experiences. It will be of interest to take a brief look at three of these groups.

113

Montanism. Montanus, the founder of this movement, was a pagan priest before his conversion to Christianity. In A.D. 157 he embarked on a crusade to correct the worldliness and rigid organization that had come to characterize the post-Apostolic Church. He sought to reintroduce into the Church the spiritual gifts that had been present in the first-century Church.

Montanism started in Asia Minor and spread rapidly throughout the Church. In A.D. 201 or 202 Tertullian, one of the most gifted Church fathers, joined the movement.

Montanism laid much emphasis on the gift of prophecy, though there are indications in the writings of Irenaeus that speaking in tongues was also found among these people. The Montanists were so convinced they were experiencing the gifts of the Spirit that they felt little need to defend these manifestations. Tertullian was a notable exception. Consequently most of the reports about the Montanists have come to us from their opponents. It is nevertheless true that some of their prophetic utterances were ill-advised. On one occasion a woman prophesied that there would shortly be war, but 13 years after her death the prediction still had not come true.

This revival group was undoubtedly started by the Holy Spirit. Unfortunately, it does not seem to have been firmly grounded in the Scriptures, with the result that some of its excesses went unchecked.

The Camisards. In 1685 the French government revoked the Edict of Nantes, which had granted religious freedom to French Protestants. From among the persecuted Protestants there emerged a group of glossolalists known originally as "The Little Prophets of the Cévennes" and later as "The Camisards." Unlike the Montanists, the Camisards were found in only a limited area of France. Several of their number went to England in 1706, where they were called "The French Prophets."

Isabeau Vincent, a young shepherdess, was the first person among the Camisards to speak in tongues. Her regional, peasant dialect was far removed from proper French. The following account that has come to us will be of interest:

For the first five weeks she spoke during her ecstasy no language but that of her country, because her only auditors were the peasantry of the village. The noise of this miracle having spread, people who understood and spoke French came to see her. She then began to speak French, with a diction as correct as if she had been brought up in the first houses of Paris. She composed admirable and excellent prayers. Her actions had no violence. Her lips moved slightly, and without the least appearance of convulsion.

Very little was written by the Camisards in defense of their unusual experiences. They undoubtedly viewed them as equivalent to the New Testament gift of tongues and were content to leave the matter at that. Their enemies viewed them as religious fanatics, and made little inquiry into the genuineness of the glossolalia and other phenomena in their midst.

The Catholic Apostolic Church. Edward Irving, the pastor of a Church of Scotland congregation in London, England, in the early 19th century, became interested in a restoration of the apostolic gifts of the Spirit. The first manifestation of the gift of tongues occurred at an early morning prayer meeting in July 1831. A few weeks later the gift of prophecy was also exercised among these Christians.

Irving was firmly convinced that the Lord was restoring to His Church the gifts of the Spirit. Unlike the Montanists or the Camisards, Irving and his followers wrote at length about the scripturalness of the phenomena they were experiencing. Irving not only appealed to the

Scriptures in defense of what was happening. He also insisted that the manifestations of the gifts in his congregation were to be in accordance with the teachings of Scripture.

Irving was eventually barred from ministering in the Church of Scotland. Shortly after his death in 1834, his followers organized the Catholic Apostolic Church. Prior to that time they were often called "Irvingites." The new church body spread throughout the British Isles, Europe, and the United States, but it is virtually non-existent today.

Paradoxically, this new organization followed a very formal liturgy in its worship. It also had men whom it called "apostles," the last of whom died in 1901. Perhaps it is more than coincidental that the present-day Pentecostal Movement started in that same year, even though there is no direct link between it and the Catholic Apostolic Church.

The Pentecostal Movement

On January 1, 1901, Agnes Ozman, a student at Bethel Bible College in Topeka, Kansas, was baptized in the Holy Spirit and spoke in tongues. This followed a period of searching the Scriptures on the assigned subject "The Batpism in the Holy Ghost," and the conclusion she and her fellow-students reached that "the indisputable proof on each occasion" of receiving the fullness of the Spirit was speaking in tongues. The significance of this event is expressed by historian Klaude Kendrick:

Although Agnes Ozman was not the first person in modern times to speak in "tongues," she was the first known person to have received such an experience as a result of specifically seeking a baptism in the Holy Spirit with the expectation of speaking in tongues. . . . For this reason the experience of Agnes Ozman is designated as the beginning of the Modern Pentecostal Revival.

The Nineteenth-Century Background. The Pentecostal Movement did not originate in a vacuum. There were several factors that prepared the way for this outpouring of the Spirit. We can touch on only a few of the most important:

1. Theological Liberalism. Many of the leading Protestant denominations were succumbing to a humanistic, naturalistic approach to Christianity which gradually stripped it of its miraculous and supernatural elements. In particular, the Bible came to be held in increasingly lower regard.

2. Cold Formalism. The religious fervor that characterized many of the churches in their earlier years had waned. Consequently even many churches that had not yet departed from the essentials the faith lacked a warmth of spirit in their worship.

3. The Holiness Movement. Within the Wesleyan (Methodist) circles, there was a desire to return to what many felt were the original teachings of John Wesley on the matter of sanctification. Consequently there arose groups that emphasized a crisis experience after salvation that was often called the baptism in the Holy Spirit, or sanctification. In addition to these, there were some in non-Wesleyan circles who also taught an experience beyond regeneration, but which also was not the Pentecostal baptism. Therefore many Christians by this time had been conditioned to believe that there could be a spiritual experience for them beyond that of regeneration. Many of the "holiness" people were filled with the Spirit and spoke in tongues when there later followed the outpouring that we know today as the Pentecostal Movement.

4. The Divine Healing Movement. Emphasis was placed by some on the power of God to heal believers in response to believing prayer. Among these leaders were men like A. B. Simpson, the founder of the Chris-

tian and Missionary Alliance, and John Alexander Dowie, the founder of the Christian Catholic Church in Zion, Illinois. Here, too, earnest believers were being prepared for the heavy emphasis the Pentecostal Movement was to place on divine healing.

Here, then, were the events that paved the way for the outpouring of the Spirit. On the one hand, there was a growing disenchantment with the established churches; on the other, a gradual preparation of hearts who were hungry for all God wished to give them.

The Sovereignty of the Holy Spirit. In addition to the foregoing, it is important to remember that God is sovereign in His dealings with men. Surely there were many spiritually hungry Christians at other times in the history of the Church. Why did God apparently reserve this outpouring until the present century? The answer certainly lies in the prophecy of Joel that God would pour out His Spirit upon all flesh in the last days (2:28, 29). Today the Church is experiencing a continuing fulfillment of that prophecy, in anticipation of the return of the Lord Jesus Christ.

Pentecostal Distinctives. Pentecostals everywhere are evangelical Protestants holding to the absolute necessity of the new birth through repentance and faith in Jesus Christ. But they differ from other evangelical churches in several important respects:

1. *The Baptism in the Holy Spirit.* This is the one distinctive doctrine of the Pentecostal Movement—the belief that subsequent to salvation a believer may be baptized in the Spirit and that this is evidenced by the initial sign of speaking in tongues. The formulation of this doctrine is largely responsible for the perpetuation of the Movement. Without the doctrine, and the accompanying experience, the Pentecostal Movement would lose its distinctiveness. Referring to this, J. Roswell

Flower, for many years a leader in the Assemblies of God, very aptly said:

There had been recorded many instances of persons speaking in tongues prior to the year 1900, but in each case the speaking in tongues was considered to be a spiritual phenomenon or at the most a "gift" of the Spirit, with the result that no particular emphasis had been given which would cause those seeking for the fullness of the Spirit to expect that they should speak in other tongues . . . . It was this decision which has made the Pentecostal Movement of the Twentieth Century.

We might add that possession of the doctrine is not sufficient; there must also be the personal reception of the experience. Yet church history amply substantiates that previous charismatic-type groups did not have such a doctrine.

2. *Charismatic Worship.* Pentecostal worship will at times be enriched by the manifestation of spiritual gifts. This is the added dimension that complements the regular elements of a service such as singing, prayer, and ministry of the Word of God. It will be used by God to meet a specific need in the life of the worshiper or the congregation as a whole.

3. *Divine Healing.* The Pentecostal Movement is in the vanguard of those who proclaim healing by God's miraculous intervention. Nowhere in the Christian Church at large is this truth preached and practiced more widely than among those who also believe in and experience the fullness of the Spirit and the manifestation of His gifts.

4. *Worldwide Evangelism.* Throughout the Church's history there have been thousands of dedicated men and women who carried the gospel to the unevangelized. The Pentecostal Movement today is expanding remarkably throughout the world. Thousands of Pentecostal missionaries and evangelists are sharing the good news of Jesus Christ. Surely the main reason for the spread

of the gospel through these instruments lies in the baptism in the Holy Spirit (Acts 1:8). The fullness of the Spirit comes to believers to empower and embolden them for the task of taking the gospel to the ends of the earth.

THE CHARISMATIC MOVEMENT

The original Pentecostal Movement was destined by God to overflow its own borders. Prior to the 1950's virtually all Christians who had experienced the Pentecostal baptism identified themselves with a Pentecostal church. Then God began to meet earnest, seeking souls from other churches, largely through the instrumentality of Pentecostal believers. Many of those newly filled with the Spirit remained in their own churches, however, sharing the joy of their new experience with their friends. In the United States alone there are today many tens of thousands of such Spirit-baptized believers. They speak of the "charismatic renewal" of the Church, and often designate themselves as the Charismatic Movement.

This movement today comprises two main groups—the neo-Pentecostals (Protestants) and the Catholic Pentecostals. In addition, many of the "Jesus people" have come into the Pentecostal experience.

There are several important lessons old-line Pentecostals can learn from their "charismatic" friends:

1. God meets earnest hearts wherever He finds them. At no time did God intend for the Pentecostal experience to be restricted only to members of the Pentecostal churches. Moses' prophetic prayer that the Lord would put His Spirit upon all His people is being answered in our day! Eldad and Medad must not, and cannot, be forbidden to prophesy (Numbers 11:27-29).

2. True unity among Christians comes only when the Holy Spirit is actively at work. Spirit-filled believers with backgrounds as diverse as Lutheran, Presbyterian, Epis-

copalian, Roman Catholic, Baptist, and Pentecostal can be united in true *koinonia*—fellowship—as together they worship the Lord in the Spirit.

3. The experience of the baptism in the Holy Spirit does not necessarily validate the doctrinal beliefs of the recipient. Some neo-Pentecostals teach baptismal regeneration—that water baptism saves a person. Among Catholic Pentecostals are those who claim that the baptism in the Spirit increased their devotion to Mary and their appreciation of the Mass. Consequently, Pentecostals cannot accept uncritically all that these friends believe. The Holy Spirit continues to work in us to unfold the meanings of the Scripture and reveal the deep things of God.

Pertinent Principles

1. The consolidation of the Pentecostal Movement was due largely to the formulation of the specific doctrine of the baptism in the Holy Spirit with the initial evidence of speaking in tongues. The Sunday school teacher has the privilege— and responsibility—of helping to perpetuate not only the doctrine but also the experience!

2. The outpouring of the Spirit is for all age groups. The spiritually sensitive teacher will be alert to opportunities to lead students into the Pentecostal experience.

3. No one can foretell how, when, or where the sovereign Spirit of God will come upon His people. But the Sunday school classroom, which is devoted largely to a study of God's Word, is an ideal place for God to manifest His presence among His people.

bibliography

Berkhof, Hendrikus, *The Doctrine of the Holy Spirit*. Richmond, Virginia: John Knox Press, 1964.

Bickersteth, Edward H., *The Holy Spirit—His Person and Work*. Grand Rapids, Michigan: Kregel Publications, 1959 (reprint edition).

Broomall, Wick, *The Holy Spirit*. Grand Rapids, Michigan: Baker Book House, 1963.

Griffith Thomas, W. H., *The Holy Spirit of God*. Grand Rapids, Michigan: Wm. B. Eerdmans Publishing House, 1963 (4th edition).

Horton, Harold. *The Gifts of the Spirit*. Bedfordshire, England: Redemption Tidings Bookroom, 1946 (2nd edition).

Kendrick Klaude, *The Promise Fulfilled*. Springfield, Missouri: Gospel Publishing House, 1961.

Morris, Leon, *Spirit of the Living God*. London, England: Inter-Varsity Press, 1960.

Nichol, John Thomas, *The Pentecostals* (formerly *Pentecostalism*). Plainfield, N. J.: Logos International, 1966, 1971.

O'Connor, Edward D., *The Pentecostal Movement in the Catholic Church*. Notre Dame, Indiana: Ave Maria Press, 1971.

Pache, Rene, *The Inspiration and Authority of Scripture*. Chicago, Illinois: Moody Press, 1969.

Packer, J. I., *"Fundamentalism" and the Word of God*. Grand Rapids, Michigan: Wm. B. Eerdmans Publishing Co., 1958.

Riggs, Ralph M., *The Spirit Himself*. Springfield, Missouri: Gospel Publishing House, 1949.

Swete, Henry B., *The Holy Spirit in the New Testament*. Grand Rapids, Michigan: Baker Book House, 1964 (reprint edition).

Synan, Vinson, *The Holiness-Pentecostal Movement in the United States*. Grand Rapids, Michigan: Wm. B. Eerdmans Publishing Co., 1971.